10 Things I Want My Son to Know

Steve Chapman

HARVEST HOUSE PUBLISHERS
Eugene, Oregon 97402

Cover by Koechel Peterson & Associates, Minneapolis, Minnesota

10 THINGS I WANT MY SON TO KNOW
Copyright © 2002 by Steve Chapman
Published by Harvest House Publishers
Eugene, Oregon 97402

Library of Congress Cataloging-in-Publication Data
   Chapman, Steve.
     10 things I want my son to know / Steve Chapman.
     p. cm.
   Includes bibliographical references.
   ISBN 0-7369-0737-8
   1. Fathers—Religious life. 2. Fatherhood (Christian theology) 3. Fathers and sons—Religious aspects—Christianity. I. Title: Ten things I want my son to know. II. Title.

BV4846.C47 2002
248.8'421—dc21   2001038510

Printed in the United States of America

06 07 / BC-CF / 10 9 8

*This book is dedicated to the two men
in this world who mean the most to me.
To my dad, P.J. Chapman, who passed his love
to me, and to my son, Nathan, who now receives
the results of that love.*

Contents

Dad—A "Soul" Provider

Have you ever stopped to ask, "Why did God give human babies a nine-month gestation period?" One reason could be that it takes that much time for a first-time father-to-be to fully realize the seriousness of what he has done and brace himself for the way his life is going to change.

Imagine finding out on a Tuesday that your wife is pregnant and on Wednesday afternoon, *bam!* the kid pops out. Emotionally it would be like driving down the interstate at 75 miles per hour and somebody dropping a brick wall on the road in your lane. Life, as you knew it, would come to an abrupt halt. In essence, it's God's grace that allows us months—not hours—to prepare for a newborn.

Even with plenty of time to reorganize our lives, when Annie's and my first child came along in March of 1977, the changes were drastic. No more spontaneous, after sunset trips to the local tennis courts to play all night (or until I could win!). No more unplanned drives to the Nashville Music Row IHOP Restaurant for a midnight pancake snack and a session of watching the weirdos. These adventures once unrestricted by the responsibilities of parenthood, became a thing of the past.

Our lifestyle experienced some serious alterations because of the coming of a baby. The decor in the spare bedroom of our duplex lost its "hippie pad" feel. The large, round, heavy, wooden telephone cable spool that we were using for a dining room table and the four milk-crate chairs were carried to the curb. There they waited to be picked up by either the city dump truck or another grateful hippie couple. In place of those pitiful items was a beautiful, borrowed crib equipped with a garage-sale mobile that played a soft lullaby as it slowly turned. The burlap curtains came down and were replaced with some nice Winnie the Pooh window treatments. These and a few other designer decorations by Fisher-Price were only a shadow of the mountain of changes we would face.

While in his infancy, my job in caring for our son was focused mainly on his body and belly. Though I did very little during this time except the gross stuff, like changing dirty diapers and catching drool drippings on my face when I held him high, I knew that eventually his soul and spirit would require my undivided attention.

When the actual "B-day" arrived, bringing with it the painful transition contractions that caused Annie to give me some really hateful looks, the shock of reality went even deeper into my formerly carefree heart. The moment Nathan's little womb-warm body met the sterile cold air of the delivery room, he cried like a…well…a baby! My first thought was, *If that's how he's gonna act, just put him back!* Annie would not have agreed to it, so I did the smart thing and kept my mouth shut.

That March morning yielded the most sobering of the changes I would have to face. I realized "our" care for him would no longer be automatic. Up until then, he had been silently mooching off his mama's meals and staying quietly out of sight. I had little to do other than enjoy his occasional kicks that I could feel as I gently palmed Annie's rounded stomach like a basketball. However, in the instant the razor sharp scissors sliced through his umbilical cord, the low-maintenance era was over. From then on, being a dad had to be voluntary and deliberate. The plethora of details required to just make sure he would be alive at the end of each day was mind (and body) boggling. Keeping him fed, cleaned, clothed, and comfortable became full-time employment for two adults.

While in his infancy, my job in caring for our son was focused mainly on his body and belly. Though I did very little during this time except the gross stuff, like changing dirty diapers and catching drool drippings on my face when I held him high, I knew that eventually his soul and spirit would require my undivided attention. It was about the time he started walking and forming intelligible words that I con-sciously added the responsibility for his spiritual growth to my list of "daddy duties."

With such an eternally serious charge staring me in the face, I was motivated to seize my chance at preparing to become his "soul" provider. I pondered the things I would want him to know, searched the Scriptures for wisdom and guidance, and leaned on veteran dads for helpful advice. (One well-seasoned father told me, "If your kids turn out smart it's because they sucked the brains out of your head. If not, they had nothing to draw from!" The good news is that nearly a quarter of a century has passed since I became a dad—and I'm still talking coherently.)

I willingly admit that I was not a perfect father. Who on earth is? When we get to heaven none of us, especially parents, are going to hear, "*Best* done thou good and faithful servant" (see Matthew 25:21). Instead, for our very best efforts, all we will get is a "*well* done." Only one Father has been flawless. Still, I believe I did do one thing right. I trusted God when He said He supplies all of our needs "according to his riches in glory by Christ Jesus" (Philippians 4:19). This is my ultimate comfort.

Compiled on the pages that follow are ten of the many "parental provisions" God was kind enough to share to help me raise a loving, God-fearing son. Though it wasn't easy to reduce the list to such a relatively small number, I have done so with two earnest wishes. One, as I relate them to you, I sincerely hope you will glean some helpful hints if you are, or hope to be, a papa. Second, I am excited about the possibility that these thoughts from my heart will be encouraging to the one person I hope will find them most useful—my own son, Nathan. If God someday chooses to bless him with the terrifyingly terrific opportunity of being a dad, perhaps he can pass some of these things on to his own kids. One thing is for sure, from personal experience I know he'll need all the help he can get!

1

You Will Always Be Mine

When God said, "This is my beloved Son, in whom I am well pleased," He said those words *about* Jesus, not *to* Him (see Matthew 3:17). Though this statement was directed to the doubtful hearts of others, they must have been music in the ears of Jesus. What was said confirmed that His Father's love for Him was neither threatened nor diminished by His humanness. The same is true for me as an earthly father. I love my son in spite of the fact that he is human!

"This is my beloved son, in whom I am well pleased." While these words were not original with me, I did borrow them when anyone came to the hospital to see our newborn. I felt somewhat unauthorized to use the divine phrase since it was first used as a reference to Jesus; however, I wanted folks to know how I felt about our new arrival and it was the best way I could think of to say it. Little did I know that my innocent usage of God's announcement regarding His own Son was so appropriate.

When the voice of the Father in heaven crossed the unseen border between eternity and time, the word He used for "son" was more than just the term humans use for their offspring (*genos*). Jesus was called God's *huios*. The same word was used in Matthew 1:21, when the angel approached Joseph in a dream and announced, "And she [Mary] shall bring forth a Son." *Huios* means "direct male issue of a person." Often it refers to one who shows maturity in acting as a son and, in Jesus' case alone, one who gives evidence of *sinless* conformity to God's character. From the very beginning, God knew His Son would act like Him. Therefore, without hesitation, the Father in heaven considered Jesus as His equal. There was no quibbling, no questions, no debate. God had confirmed it before Jesus' birth, and He settled it once and for all at the Jordan River: "This is my beloved Son."

When I smiled and used that adopted phrase, I didn't know that in essence I was saying, "This kid is going to be an exact replica of his papa." Not only was it true that Nathan physically favored me (in that he was a human with arms, legs, eyes, etc.), he would reflect my character. The major difference was that unlike Jesus, who acted like His *holy* Father, the example my son had to follow was not so saintly.

I claim him as my son in spite of the fact that, just like his dad, he was also born a sinner. My affection for him is not based on performance or the lack of it.

As it turned out, unfortunately, Nathan *was* indeed just like his "old man." (I fully deserve that title because it is used to describe the sinful nature of humans in Ephesians 4:22 and Romans 6:6.) With hardly any extra effort, Nathan became a duplicate of the "old man" in his dad. The fact that he mirrored my fallen nature was all the more reason to regard him as my son. To be honest, I felt sorrow for him that such fleshly weakness had been passed on. Even though he had inherited a propensity to sin, it did not lessen my resolve to embrace him. It strengthened it. He would need my love even more because of it.

With that as the backdrop, I can truly say that of the ten things I want Nathan to know and never forget, number one is that *my love for him is unconditional.* I claim him as my son in spite of the fact that, just like his dad, he was born a sinner. There is nothing he can ever do to change my heart on this issue. My affection for him is not based on his performance or lack of it. I love him because he is me in another body, so to speak.

Of course, it didn't take too long into his infancy before my level of love for him was challenged. His first act of testing my resolve took place within minutes of getting home from the hospital and walking through the front door. Without permission he filled his little britches with the most awful, foul-smelling stuff imaginable. Convinced he was broken, I seriously considered taking him back to the hospital for repairs. I wondered how on earth a creature as sweet as our newborn could be so capable of emitting something so gross. His infantile deposits had a man-sized rank. What's worse, he did it quite often.

I suppose it is out of the kindness of God that new dads have to deal with baby poop. It is a physical, fair warning about the spiritual condition of the child. By the time a kid reaches the toddler years, most parents have been sufficiently trained to have a certain level of patience and understanding when it comes to being dumped on by their offspring. The resilience that is developed in a young mother and father will serve them well as their child's teen years approach.

Dads should also be glad that God, in His awesome wisdom, did not make human baby sinners able to immediately stand, like ponies and fawns do. Perhaps He didn't do it because He knew they would quickly run to destructive behavior. For whatever reason, God didn't design children that way—and we can certainly be thankful. Imagine what amount of damage could be done by uncontrolled, walking human babies. The valuable trinkets sitting vulnerably on coffee tables would never survive the first full day with them around. (That trauma comes later, when the parents have had plenty of time to childproof their dwelling.) In the slip-of-the-tongue words of our neighbor, Kathy, who has four children seven years and younger, when it comes to kids and household valuables, the Scripture to remember is: "*Chain up a child when he is young...!*" (Check out Proverbs 22:6.)

His answer revealed a level of intelligence and reasoning that frightened both of us...and has kept us up at night for years!

By the time Nathan was three years old he had sufficiently tested the strength of my love for him. He didn't need to do anything extra, but he did. When Nathan was barely into his fourth year, he came into the house one summer day dragging a heavy, full-size hammer. That sight is never good to behold, especially if the look on the child's face has the troubling expression of mischief written on it.

When we asked him what he had been doing with the hammer, he innocently told us, "I *bwoke* out the windows!"

Asking him to explain what he had actually done was a risky thing to do for our nerves that were already frayed; however, we found the bravery to enquire. He took us outside to show us how he had used the hammer to tap all of our basement windows until they made that "tinkling" sound. When we asked him why he would have done such a terrible thing, his answer revealed a level of intelligence and reasoning that frightened both of us.

"You never told me not to."

That response has kept us up at night for years wondering about all the other things we failed to tell him not to do!

The opportunities to prove my incontestable love for Nathan did not stop with the hammer and "bwoke" glass affair. When he got older, torturing his sister and justifying his actions with a twisted interpretation of Proverbs 17:17 wore at my will to love him consistently. He would try to convince me that he had a biblical mandate to torment Heidi. "Dad, doesn't the Scripture say 'a brother is born for adversity'? That means I *have to* give her grief! Right?" His clever attempt to rewrite the rules amazed me. He really was like his "old man." Shucks!

Then there were the occasional "sassy mouth, disrespectful explosions" toward his mother. That one really put some weight on the sinister side of my scales. Rarely did I raise my voice in anger, but when my sweetheart was violated in such a way, I found it within me to blow it out. I could not tolerate my child's mistreatment of the woman who had gone to the jaws of death to give him life.

It was around the time when the dust had settled on the basement windows disaster, that I wrote a song for Nathan. I wanted to musically document my determination to love him in the face of such encounters with his humanness. The most important thing I could say to my sin-prone child is contained in the following lyric:

You Will Always Be Mine

You were born to me, I was there
And I remember your mother's pain
And I was very proud
To let you have my name
And I want you to know
Wherever you go
Or whatever you do
If you're the president or a prisoner
You are my child
And I will always love you

You will always be mine
And you can lean on me anytime
Whatever you do I will always love you
You will always be mine

And I'm living for the day
When I hear you say
"Daddy, I've been born again."
And the Savior will tell you
What I'm telling you now
'Cause I got the words from Him

He'll be saying, "You will always be mine.
And you can lean on me anytime
Whatever you do
I will always love you
You will always be mine."[1]

Call Him "Son"

If there was one failure I was determined to avoid as a dad, it was that Nathan would never hear me call him "son." For some mysterious reason, all can seem well with the world when a man is confident that his father unconditionally loves and accepts him. Down through the ages of time, men's spirits have risen or fallen on the knowledge that their fathers either proudly called them sons or refused or neglected to do so.

One of the most impacting examples of this is found in the story a woman told us of the time her husband stood at the bedside of his dying father. As his dad writhed in the final minutes of pain, he suddenly bolted upright in his bed and screamed, "What's happening to me, Son?"

With that, the distraught husband ran out of the room weeping. His wife followed him into the hall and consoled him, "Honey, it must be awful to see your dad dying this way."

His sob-filled response to his caring wife was not what she expected. "That's not why I'm crying. It's because that's the first time he's ever called me 'son'!"

The dad had waited far too long. What a shame that it was in his nearly unconscious state that he finally provided something so simple yet so desperately desired by his son. The dad probably died without knowing what an extreme mixture of sadness and joy the moment had yielded. Like a man who was drowning in the raging waters of emotion and needing a life preserver, the son will cling tightly to the last words of his father for the rest of his days. How much better his time on earth would have been had the title of "son" been tenderly spoken years earlier.

I don't want to make the same mistake. For that reason, I never passed up an opportunity to tell Nathan that he was loved and that even when he failed my love would remain true. I wanted to be like my friend who revealed how to show unconditional love. He told me that his boy was quite shy but was very talented at playing the drums. One day he surprised his folks when he announced he had joined the percussion line of the high-school marching band. They were shocked and happy that their normally reserved son had taken the initiative to do something so outgoing. The first Friday football game finally arrived, and my friend said that he and his wife nervously climbed into the bleachers. Halftime came at last and the dad said, "Steve, his mom and I were so excited when the band marched out onto the field and began their program. We were never more proud of our son that night. We looked down on the field and the whole band was going the wrong way...except for our boy!"

Though the dad's humorous story didn't contain an ounce of fact, the truth in it is profound. We need to be proud of our children. I, for one, will be forever grateful that my mother and father showed a great deal of mercy and undying love to me, even in the face of all the times I fell "out of step" with their hopes for my life. I admit that, at times, I was a source of embarrassment to them, yet I can still recall their countenance of acceptance.

One of those instances involved a night they got a phone call from a neighbor who lived directly behind them one street over. She warned my folks, "You all lock your doors! There's a crazy, long-haired man walking up and down the street playing a guitar and singing at the top of his lungs. It's scaring me to death. I just thought you ought to know in case he comes your way!"

Much to their chagrin, the crazy man was their son, and they knew it. They didn't try to explain to their neighbor that she need not be alarmed. They simply bowed their heads and offered one more prayer for their boy who had climbed too far out on the limb of weirdness.

While I certainly provided my mother and father with plenty of other opportunities to express unconditional love, my contributions to their challenge returned to me. Nathan made sure of it. While none of his antics were life threatening or potentially ruinous to the family name, I won't confess them here. (I'll let him do that in the book he'll write someday.) I can only hope that each time I remind him of my love and acceptance, the words strengthen and comfort him in his heart the way my parents' generous love did for me.

Is It Too Late?

It would be fair at this point to recognize that not all men who want to express their unconditional love do well at *saying* it. Instead, they do much better by *showing* it, much like the father in the following song.

Love Was Spoken

Before the sun came up, daddy rolled out of bed
He'd go to work, that's how love was said
He'd spend the money that he made all week
To feed a hungry family, that's how love would
   speak

Love was spoken, though daddy rarely used the
   words
Love was spoken, in everything he did, love was
   all we heard.

On Saturday morning when a man ought to rest
Dad would work on the house and that's how
   love was said
When Sunday came we were off to the chapel
Love was spoken so pure and simple

Saying love did not come easy
But we did not criticize
'Cause we could hear him say he loved us
When we'd listen with our eyes.

Love was spoken though daddy rarely used the
    words
Love was spoken, in everything he did
Love was all we heard[2]

I wrote this lyric many years ago to come to the aid of
men who are good fathers but lack the verbal skills to express
the deepest feelings in their hearts. The dad in the song is to
be commended for his devotion to display affection even
though he struggled with saying it. Furthermore, the son did
very well to graciously accept this unspoken love. However,
I cannot let the "silent type" of dad totally off the hook. I
strongly caution that we men must understand that
absolutely nothing warms the heart of a son more than
hearing his father say, "You're mine, I love you, and I'm proud
of you!"

Furthermore, these words are mysteriously encouraging.
So much so that a man's very confidence is impacted by it.
When Jesus, for example, was about to do the humbling job
of washing the disciples' feet, Scripture records an interesting
statement: "Jesus, *knowing that the Father had given all things
into His hands,* and that He had come forth from God and
was going back to God, got up from supper, and laid aside
His garments; and taking a towel, He girded Himself. Then
He poured water into the basin and began to wash the disciples' feet and to wipe them with the towel" (John 13:3-5
NASB, emphasis added). How could the Son of God be so
unthreatened by doing something so lowly? Because He had
no doubt about His status with His Father. That confidence

allowed Him to see that service did not lessen His royalty—
it highlighted it!

There are sons who have never received the kind of
audible acceptance Jesus knew from His Father. Many of
them are afraid to attempt something as remarkable as humbling themselves and serving another human being. Why?
Perhaps it's because they are preoccupied with trying to find
acceptance and bolster their own self-worth.

Like medicine, a father's words of acceptance can heal a
son's wounded ego. *Showing* it and *saying* it should go hand
in hand.

Is it too late for dads to openly express love to children
who are grown to eye level? Absolutely not. In the soil of
human hearts, sowing word seeds of love in the autumn of a
son's life still yields a good crop. Let me illustrate.

I eat, drink, and breathe deer hunting. Well, maybe not
quite—but it's close! I own a 20-acre piece of property that I
hunt on. There were plenty of signs (deer tracks and trails)
that made it clear the critters were using my woods to get
from one field to another, but the absence of plenty of drop-
pings and impressions in the leaves on the forest floor that
would reveal their resting there said to me that my woods
was a hallway and not a bedroom for them.

I was not raised on a farm, so I didn't know the full facts
about seeding and harvest times. Without that knowledge, it
was natural for me to assume that because it wasn't until
August when I realized my need for a food plot to attract
deer, it was too late to do something about it. Then one day
I was standing in the aisle of a local hunting goods store when
I saw a bag of seed with large letters printed on the label.
They read: "Good for fall planting." Upon closer inspection,
I found these words, "Best results if planted in mid-August to
mid-September." *Whoa!*

When I got home with my bag of seeds, I excitedly announced my find to Annie, my farmer's daughter wife and expert gardener.

"Sure!" she said. "Anyone knows there are lots of seeds you can put in the ground later in the year. Some of my best flowers are planted in the fall."

I nursed my outdoorsman ego and then promptly headed to my property to start clearing a large area of the woods. My goal was to entice the local whitetail to stop in for breakfast and stay a spell (while I waited for them in my permanently mounted treestand!). As I was removing rocks and other debris out of the ground in preparation to plow and plant my "fall blend," I suddenly thought of dads who have assumed that because so much time has passed, it is too late to sow seeds of love into their grown kid's hearts. I thought of what good news it would be for them to know the truth that it is never too late to make a call or write a letter of love to a child. The fruit that it can bear, even in the autumn of a child's life, is sweet. I pray that if this is your situation you will find the courage to sow some love seeds as soon as possible.

Nathan now towers above me in height. His features are that of a mature man. Yet I still proudly use the phrase, "This is my beloved son, in whom I am well pleased." When I do, I detect the same childlike expression of pleasure on his face that was there when I affirmed this truth to him in his much younger days. For the sake of sons of all ages, I suggest you give these famous words a try. Though they belong to God, I really don't think He will mind. After all, He is a Father, too!

2

Proof of My Love

"For he who does wrong will receive the consequences of the wrong which he has done, and that without partiality" (Colossians 3:25). When I put my son's face in the frame of this passage I am shaken to the very core of my soul. Knowing he will surely stand before God and give an account for his behavior motivates me to do all I can to help him find God's favor in that hour. And the one thing that will accomplish that goal is the hardest thing a father has to do—discipline his son.

Saying to my son that he is loved was the first and most important thing I could do as a young father. I knew I had to be as careful to verbalize my acceptance of Nathan as I was to provide food and shelter. Not one tangible need supplied by my hands would compare to the value of the invisible provision that came from my heart. Even with the right words spoken, though, there were moments when my offerings of love seemed to be totally ineffective in motivating him to good behavior. What I had to do when his sinful nature openly erupted was not pleasant for either of us. But if I didn't do it I knew it would eventually signal that I didn't really care. With that in mind, the second thing I want my son to know is that the sure proof of my love for him had to sometimes be shown through the painful administering of discipline.

Deputized by Proverbs 13:24, I loved my son with the paddle of reproof. The passage reads: "He who withholds his rod hates his son, but he who loves him disciplines him diligently" (NASB). Having had my own experience with my folks not sparing the rod of correction, I can only wish that the last word in that passage could have been spelled "deal-a-gently." Unfortunately, there is hardly any way to render the rod without appearing to be anything but gentle. But there is an incredibly important purpose for the discipline administered by an earthly father. Borrowing another valuable illustration from the world of seeds and soil, this one clearly defines the eternal benefits of being careful to correct a child's behavior when they are young.

In Luke 8:5, it is noted that as a farmer sowed seeds, they fell into various types of soil. Some seeds fell along the road where they were trampled under the feet of passersby and birds ate them. Other seeds were lost in the dry, rocky soil. And some were choked out by thorns. The seeds that landed in "good soil" yielded an abundant crop.

During one of the episodes of disciplining Nathan, this passage came to me and I believe I heard from the Lord about it. Soil is made good and sowable only by tilling it and clearing it of worthless debris. Once the ground is prepared properly, the seeds have a safe and healthy place to germinate. Discipline is basically the act of tilling a child's heart so that when God's Word, the incorruptible seed, is sown it will take root and grow. The following lyric was written during this time in my life as a father.

The Farmer and the Field

I was doing something bad when I got caught
And I won't forget the lesson that my daddy taught

He said, "What I gotta do, Son, it's gonna be
   hard."
And it felt like a plow going through my heart

'Cause he was the farmer and I was the field
And it always hurt when the ground was tilled
But he was getting rid of the rocks and the weeds
So the ground would be good when he sowed the
   seed

Well, my daddy was right, it didn't feel so good
And I would've run away if I could
But then he put his arms around me as the tears
   came down
I didn't know it but those tears would be helping
   the ground

Well, my daddy's not around anymore
But I can hear those words now and then
'Cause I gave my heart to the heavenly Father
Now He's got the plow in His hands
And I've come to understand

That He is the farmer and I am the field
And it's always gonna hurt when the ground is
   tilled
But He's just getting rid of the rocks and the weeds
So the ground will be good when He sows the seed[3]

Disciplining is one of the strangest dichotomies I had to
face as a dad. I didn't think about it much (if any) when I was
under my father's disciplinary hand. However, when I con-
fronted the task of dishing out pain to my own beloved,
tender, little picture of myself, it was an entirely different
matter. Suddenly the old adage, "This is going to hurt me

worse than it will hurt you" had real meaning. But I knew if I loved Nathan I would follow through. And so I did.

How utterly odd it felt the first time I showed love to him by causing him pain. Nathan's tiny tears watered my eyes. His crying literally made my chest hurt. The temporary sting on his young derriere left a permanent mark on my heart. It is there today, testifying of my love for my son.

The idea of rendering pain to a child in order to help them connect wrong choices with consequences has waned in its acceptance. There are those who equate spanking with child abuse. That's why it's important to be calm and reasonable in administering correction. Since the object of this reproof is to change behavior, a wise dad will avoid publicly paddling a child because it adds unnecessary shame and embarrassment that can permanently scar a child's spirit. If you do have to administer a spanking in a public setting, go to a remote corner of the store or a bathroom for privacy.

The time had come when spanking was no longer appropriate. I had to discover other means to his "end."

I also suggest that dads not use their bare hands to spank a child. The "rod" of correction is what a child should fear, not the dad. I have been guilty in the past of doing what a lot of dads do when there is unbridled chaos going on in the backseat of the car. After putting up with their children's bickering and taunting long enough, dads sometime reach over the backseat and, while looking straight ahead at the road, perform the "random spanking" technique. As they wildly swing their arms in an attempt to connect with the tender flesh that houses the meanness behind them, they growl in anger. To the children, this type of reaction identifies the behavior with the parent instead of with the inappropriate behavior.

When my boy was little enough to be able to walk upright under the kitchen table without banging his head, discipline wasn't that difficult. A light spanking on the meaty part of his rear end with one of Annie's wooden, lightweight kitchen spatulas was all it took. However, when the day came that he was so big he could barely slide his knees under that same table, discipline became a different matter. As my son grew closer to me in height, I learned that the pain of correction had to take a different form. Because the time had come when spanking was no longer appropriate, I had to discover other means to his "end." A good example of altering my methods came one morning in his thirteenth year.

He had ignored several of his mother's attempts to wake him up for school so he could get ready to ride with his sister. It was nearly past the time to make the ten-minute drive when Annie came to me, frazzled by the sleepy grunts he made when she tried again to rouse him.

Instead of forcing him out of bed, I decided to let him sleep. I took Heidi on to school that morning, returned home, and waited. About nine o'clock he came blasting out of his bedroom in a panic.

In a flash he was dressed and standing at the front door. I walked by and he reluctantly asked, "Dad, are you going to take me to school?"

I answered, "No, Son. I've already been there once this morning. You'll have to get to school the best way you can."

"But what about the English test I'm supposed to take?"

"Too bad, Nate. I'm sorry. I suggest you call a taxi."

He stood motionless, terrified at the thought of flunking the English test because he wasn't there. Finally, in a low, tentative voice, he asked, "Dad, how much would a taxi cost me?"

"Oh, probably four or five bucks," I answered.

With a slight stutter, he asked, "Will you take me for that much?"

I thought about it for a moment and answered, "I suppose."

I did take him—and I took his money. The stop at McDonalds for coffee that morning was compliments of some of the hardest earned pennies a fellow can spend. I had spanked Nathan in his wallet, and the pain was intense.

The outward evidence of a child's inner attitude of rebellion can be a horrid thing for any dad to face.

Confrontations like that aren't easy. How true it is that "all discipline for the moment seems not to be joyful, but sorrowful; yet to those who have been trained by it, afterwards it yields the peaceful fruit of righteousness" (Hebrews 12:11 NASB). Though it was difficult, I was motivated to follow through by my desire to see God's Word firmly planted in the soil of Nathan's heart. I tried to follow the Lord's instructions by being faithful to *afflict* him when necessary (see Psalm 119:75).

I am thankful that Nathan didn't always resist the discipline. Because I consistently reaffirmed my love for him with words and deeds, he trusted my judgment when corrective measures had to be taken. I'll never forget what he said when he came home from school on the day I served as his taxi ride. When I apologized for having to punish him, he responded with, "Oh, Dad! That wasn't punishment; that was a lesson." I was proud of his insightful reaction and, amazingly, for almost three weeks it didn't happen again!

Though Nathan had a spirit that was pliable, there were times when he seriously struggled to follow the admonition in Proverbs 3:11: "My son, do not reject the discipline of the LORD, or loathe His reproof" (NASB). His resistance to correction was sometimes displayed by rolling his eyes or mumbling complaints accompanied by major sulking. As I sought to know what to do in those cases, I came to a revelation that literally changed my life as a dad. In order to maintain my role as a loving and diligent disciplinarian throughout those eye-to-eye years, I had to learn not to be afraid of my growing son.

The outward evidence of a child's inner attitude of rebellion can be a horrid thing for any dad to face. I found the courage to confront it by leaning on the wisdom found in Philippians 1:28. It reveals that displaying peace in the face of an opponent is a sign of defeat for them. I had to understand, of course, that in times of heavy defiance, my son was not the enemy, that it was his sinful nature that was the combatant. Loving the sinner and hating the sin is easier to do when Ephesians 6:12 is remembered: "For our struggle is not against flesh and blood, but against the...spiritual forces of wickedness." Psalm 51:5 is tough enough to admit for myself, but to apply it to my son was even harder: "Behold, I was brought forth in iniquity, and in sin my mother conceived me." Ephesians 2:3 accurately describes us when it affirms that we are "by nature children of wrath." While my son's tendency to be a transgressor was undeniable, I couldn't let it keep me from doing the right thing. Knowing in advance that his rebellious nature would occasionally surface was a great help in being emotionally prepared to confront disobedience. Because I loved him, I refused to be afraid of his reaction. That composure calmed a lot of storms.

I admit that it would have been much easier to walk away from him when his "flesh" was overpowering his spirit. The emotion-packed confrontations could have been smoothly avoided by simply letting the trespass go unchecked. His bliss and my safe blood pressure would have been maintained. However, something far more important than my son's temporary happiness was at stake. It was the eternal condition of his soul that kept my shoulder to the wheel of correction.

Facing the Guilt

Dads often shrink back from engaging in discipline for at least two reasons—both of which involve guilt. They may feel guilty because of their absences. Whether by choice or out of necessity, when a father is too much out of the picture of his kids' lives, it is very awkward for him to enter back in and regain the right to discipline. I'll never forget the day that Nathan shocked me into reality with his assessment of my presence...or lack of it.

I had been on a very long tour with a music group I was a part of. Our schedule took us out west for more than 20 days. It was one of many trips that had severed my ability to interact with my son. When our 40-foot rig rolled onto our street, I was elated to see my little family. I had been home just a few hours when Nathan did something I didn't think was appropriate conduct. Without realizing I had become somewhat of a stranger to him, I administered the rod of correction.

Without batting either of his little three-year-old eyes, Nathan suggested, "Old man, won't you get in that motor home and go on another trip."

I was shattered to the very core of my being. I realized that while I was "out there" encouraging others to strengthen their walk with Christ, I had forfeited the right to be my son's authority figure. It was in that very moment that I began to rehearse my resignation speech, which I made not long after the incident. I had come to grips with the truth that absence does not make the heart grow fonder—at least not when it comes to dads and sons.

Not only can the guilt of absence tamper with a dad's right to discipline, the guilt of sin is another real hindrance. Many scholars agree that the psalmist David, for example, may have cowered at the idea of confronting the sins of his boys because he felt guilty for his own immoral tryst with Bathsheba and the murder of her husband, Uriah. For whatever reason, David could not deal effectively with his own sons. He would have done well to bravely face the ugly behavior of his boys as recorded in 2 Samuel (beginning at chapter 13). Instead, he turned his head away from the ungodly actions of Amnon, who raped his half sister, then ignored Absalom's vengeful murder of Amnon. The outcome was not only David's loss of one son, but also the wedge that was driven between himself and Absalom. Eventually, David tragically lost both sons to untimely deaths.

If it is true that David's shame for his own sin blocked his willingness to discipline, it makes it even more ironic that from his own pen came the best instructions for every dad in terms of how to regain (or maintain) the courage, as well as the right, to discipline. His wisdom is found in Psalm 51, a passage often titled "A Contrite Sinner's Prayer for Pardon."

It is David's cry for forgiveness after he realized his sin with Bathsheba. Consider the following:

> Be gracious to me, O God, according to Your lovingkindness; according to the greatness of Your compassion blot out my transgressions. Wash me thoroughly from my iniquity and cleanse me from my sin. For I know my transgressions, and my sin is ever before me. Against You, You only, I have sinned and done what is evil in Your sight, so that You are justified when You speak and blameless when You judge....Purify me with hyssop, and I shall be clean; wash me, and I shall be whiter than snow....Hide Your face from my sins and blot out all my iniquities. Create in me a clean heart, O God, and renew a steadfast spirit within me. Do not cast me away from Your presence and do not take Your Holy Spirit from me. Restore to me the joy of Your salvation and sustain me with a willing spirit" (verses 1-4,7,9-12).

Verse 13 begins with a word that is in italics in the NASB, indicating it is not in the original language, but rightly implied. The word is "then." The placement of this word holds the key to the right timing for a dad's disciplining of a child. Following David's thorough and sincere repentance, he says, "*Then* I will teach transgressors Your ways." This seems to illustrate that it is *after* a dad has made things right with the Lord that he will be both qualified and enthusiastic about guiding his "little transgressors" to the righteous ways of God. A guilt-ridden dad often feels powerless and, as a result, hesitant to punish. A good dose of forgiveness will always strengthen a father who admits he has been weakened by sin.

To help you remember this divine order for dads, listen closely the next time you fly on a commercial airliner. Before the plane leaves the ground, a flight attendant gives the required safety speech. Part of it is something similar to this: "In the unlikely event of a loss of cabin pressure, a panel above you will open and an oxygen mask will drop out of the ceiling. Take the mask, put it over your nose and mouth, adjust it with the tabs, and breathe normally." (Is hyperventilating considered normal?)

What is usually said next is directed to parents. The attendant will often say, "If you have a child with you, first put the mask on yourself, *then* assist your child." At that moment a great biblical truth has been illustrated. The adult *has to be the one* who is conscious before he can help the young one. When we go to Christ, cast our cares on Him, and take in the life-giving "oxygen" of His pardon for our sins, we can then be effective fathers.

Remember my confrontations with Nathan? Even though he was too young to understand, I inflicted the painful consequences of disobedience on my son in order to say, "I love you, and you will always be mine." In God's eyes, discipline is one of the grandest forms of loving acceptance. Proverbs 3:12 reminds us, "For whom the LORD loves He reproves, even as a father corrects the son in whom he delights." And Hebrews 12:10 reveals the long-term benefit of being diligent to discipline: "For they [our earthly fathers] disciplined us for a short time as seemed best to them, but He disciplines us for our good, so that we may share His holiness."

Though he will always be my son, today Nathan's heart belongs to the Lord. I can only hope that the efforts I took at tilling the field of his heart through the years has made it easier for him to accept his heavenly Father's discipline.

Nathan has made me proud and, without reservation, to all who will listen I say: "He is my only begotten son, in whom I am well pleased!"

3

Good Work

Let the favor of the Lord our God be upon us; and con-
firm for us the work of our hands; yes, confirm the work
of our hands.

PSALM 90:17

One of the things I could hardly wait to tell my son was that God had more for him to do with his life than to just occupy (a messy) space and rid the world of excess hamburgers. I wanted him to know that he has a divinely appointed purpose, that his steps are ordered by the Lord (see Psalm 37:23 NKJV). I was also excited to let him know that he is "created in Christ Jesus for good works, which God prepared beforehand, that [he] should walk in them (Ephesians 2:10 NKJV). What a joy it was to inform my son that his good deeds had the potential to bring glory to Christ in the same way a delicious apple compliments the tree from which it came.

Included in the implications of the word for "work," *ergon* in the original language, is the idea of good deeds as used in Ephesians 2:10 *and* a person's occupation. Even a person's daily job can be used to glorify God. While I knew that a chosen vocation can never bring about the salvation of his soul, I did understand that when a person truly appreciates his redemption through Christ, everything he does becomes an opportunity to testify of that salvation— including his work. A person who approaches his job with that attitude often makes a great employee! Not only is he usually a "hard worker," but he is also a "heart worker." He is motivated to excellence in the work place because he wants to honor the one who's name is Excellent!

With hopes that Nathan would want to "do all to God's glory," I considered it a wonderful opportunity as a dad to help him discover a work his hands could perform that might glorify his Father in heaven. As anxious as I was to begin that search, however, there was a very important beginning step that had to be taken.

His mother and I knew that in order for our son to be qualified to *do* the good works, he needed to first *accept* the gift of the *completed work of the crucified and risen Christ*. By establishing a relationship with God's only begotten Son, our child would have a connection with the heavenly Father through Christ that would allow him to better understand God's will. For that reason, as soon as Nathan seemed to have the capacity to understand the message of salvation, Annie and I began to sow that seed in his heart.

One of the things that helped him grasp the idea that he was a sinner with a need for forgiveness was the discipline we covered in chapter 2. By the diligent reminders through discipline that wrong choices resulted in painful consequences, Nathan slowly figured out that he did indeed have the tendency to transgress. At a very early age the light came on in his heart, and he understood his need for Christ.

It was an unforgettable day when Nathan encountered the Lord's divine forgiveness. We were traveling in Texas on a concert tour. He was five years old at the time. As we drove along a rural highway we spotted a fruit stand, and our mouths watered at the sight of the huge oranges that were displayed. We pulled over and browsed the tables that were heaped with various kinds of juicy fruit. Next to each type was a bowl of presliced samples for the customers to try.

_____

With the foundation of salvation laid in his heart, we had a place to build the understanding that God would reveal the work He had prepared beforehand for him to do.

_____

We made our purchase and headed down the highway. We had driven about 45 minutes when Nathan came to the front of the van in tears. His little heart pounded with fear as he confessed that he had taken some of the slices and had not paid for them. Annie and I quickly realized he didn't understand that the samples were free for the taking. As far as he was concerned he had stolen the fruit.

The dilemma we faced was whether or not to convince him that he had not done wrong or to let guilt do its necessary work in his heart. We knew very well that the latter would require a long drive back to the fruit stand so he could admit his wrongdoing to the lady at the cash register. Not caring that it would sound ridiculous to most, we opted to turn around and go the added miles for the sake of Nathan's sensitive soul. Thankfully, we had the time to do it.

When we returned to the stand, Nathan nervously got out, approached the lady, and made his confession. She looked at us understandingly and smiled as she assured our son that he was forgiven and that no harm was done. With a relieved bounce in his step he returned to the van feeling like a new kid.

As we once again headed toward our concert commitment, Annie pulled Nathan up onto her lap and explained the feelings of "godly sorrow" that he had experienced. Then she taught him about God's provision of cleansing from our sins through His Son's sacrifice on the cross, that Jesus was raised from the dead, and that He now offers each of us eternal life. Nathan listened closely as his mother informed him that we could not be saved by our own works but only by what Christ had done. He cried as he prayed a sinner's prayer. The fruit that was born in his spirit that day was sweet.

With the foundation of salvation laid in his heart, we then had a place to build the understanding that in his years ahead God would reveal the work He had "prepared beforehand" for him to do. If I had known what God had in mind concerning my son's eventual vocation, I would have enrolled him in the best school available that could teach him all he needed to know about that skill. That kind of foreknowledge was not granted to me. Instead, I felt like I was throwing darts at a target I couldn't see when it came to guidance in this area. Eventually, I decided the best thing to do was to carefully and closely observe any natural gifts my son possessed and cultivate any talents he seemed to have. I would do so believing by faith that God would lead me—and him—to the vocation He had chosen.

To accomplish this, one of the first steps I took was to limit toys and be generous with tools. As it was, I had plenty of late night, painful, one foot hops through the darkness of the hallways after stepping barefooted on one of the many G.I. Joe figures or Matchbox cars. While Nathan (and I!) enjoyed these items, they seemed to do little more than entertain him. Fostering a vivid imagination in little boys with little toys has its merits, but I knew he would quickly come to the day when he would have to "put away childish things." Why not give him a head start? For that reason I was excited when my son began to show some motor and mental skills with some of the tools of my trade. I started handing used equipment down to him. In my case, it was musical instruments and recording machines.

When he was nearly ten years old I noticed he had an interest in the guitar. His young fingers were unusually long, and their movement showed dexterity. With that in mind, I made plans to surprise him at Christmas with his own guitar. By the time December came he had already learned a few chords on my Gibson, but it was oversized for him. When he opened his gift and found a guitar that fit him perfectly he was genuinely excited. As we plugged it into the amp, I said, "Son, your job is to learn to play that thing." And that he did.

What transpired over the next 6 years helped me gain a new appreciation for Jesus' prayer found in John 17:4: "I glorified You on the earth, having accomplished the work which You have given Me to do." By the time Nathan was 16, he was so far beyond me in his ability to play the guitar that it made me wonder if he really was my own son. (Maybe that older dad was right. My child had indeed sucked the brains right out of my head!) While a serious guitarist like my son would never say he has completed the learning process, he has certainly fulfilled my expectations.

To this day I am immensely impressed with his prowess on the guitar. I know it sounds parentally obnoxious to say, but whenever I hear him play it makes me think he could have easily filled the role of the psalmist David when his music soothed the heart of King Saul. If God has chosen Nathan's "guitartistry" as one of the good works he is to walk in, I will delight in knowing that I assisted in developing it.

Nathan's interest and development of guitar playing gave birth to another potential good work. I discovered that he had an uncanny ability to write song lyrics. At around the age of 11, he handed me a poem he had written for his sister as a birthday gift. Having no money to his name, he opted to give Heidi the written version of his deepest feelings about her. ("Plus," he said, "it's really cheap!") Here's an excerpt:

> Here's to my sister, remember every day
> No matter what I've said, here's what I'd like to say
> I will always love you, be with you to the end
> When no one else is around, I will be your friend.[4]

My fatherly assessment of his poetic prowess was tempered by my professional opinion, and I saw great potential. I began to encourage him to pursue lyric composition. Through the years he has done just that. A later lyric shows great maturity as well as the craftsmanship of a true wordsmith. Nathan adapted the following from Psalm 77:16-18.

Only Trembling

> The earthquake shakes the ground
> The thunder claps its sound
> The lightning throws its arrows
> Cloud's tears fall all around
> Tell me why this happens
> Why the earth acts so unkind

All of nature is only trembling
Before the Lord Most High

Only trembling, only bowing
On its knees before God
All of nature cowers at His awesome
    power
Only trembling before God

But we all shake our fists
And go our own way
And we laugh at all that's holy
And we use His name in vain
But shouldn't we take notice
Of how the earth is so humbled?
And listen to the sounds
As frightened ground rumbles

It's only trembling, only bowing
On its knees before God
All of nature cowers at His awesome
    power
Only trembling before God.[5]

One other talent that might have remained buried was uncovered when I started giving Nathan some of our used recording equipment. He possessed an outstanding ability to understand "signal path" (the directions electronic signals follow as they mysteriously go from the performer to the microphone, from the mixer to the blank tape, and then to the monitor speakers).

Allowing Nathan to learn how to operate the very high-dollar recorders, which we used to produce major projects, had a significant cost attached. In order to put his hands on the newer, expensive equipment, he was first allowed to experiment on some of the older but still valuable machines. Although some of these found their way to the electronic graveyard, the price was worth what was gained. Nathan is a very professional engineer and producer. This high-tech talent may very well prove to be included in one of the "good works" in God's plan for him.

He must be allowed the freedom to choose
to follow God's work order.

Through the years there have been other discoveries of giftedness in my son. To name two, his eye for taking beautiful, jaw-dropping photographs caught us by surprise. Also, writing song lyrics was a springboard to publishing a book that focuses on another area of interest—hiking.

With all his capabilities that have been mined, I am very much aware that none of these skills may represent the vocational field Nathan will ultimately plow. I have no problem with this possibility—and it would be foolish to feel otherwise. To demand that he hoe only the music row might do nothing more than build a wall between his heart and his obedience to his heavenly Father. Nathan must be allowed the freedom to choose to follow *God's* work order. I can only trust that I have done right in redeeming the time by actively searching out my son's gifts. If nothing else was accomplished on my part, by placing on a young, energetic fellow the responsibility that comes with tools (instead of toys) I managed to keep a teenager away from the time-wasteful halls of the local mall. That in itself, I'm sure, has pleased the Lord.

A Man's Work

I want my son to know that God honors the work of a man's hands. Consider, for example, some of the items that were used by Jesus when He walked this planet in the flesh: a manger, a ship, a robe, a table, a pair of sandals, a basket, and even a cross. With His touch, things that men and women labored to manufacture became tools used to mark the presence of the Son of God. While those whose hands did the work might have done so to make a living, God had a higher purpose in mind for their goods.

The same is true today. For instance, my dad provided for our family by toiling in an aluminum plant for 27 years. It might not be known until we get to heaven what impact his contribution to the fabrication of metal may have had on the grand scheme of things. Perhaps there is an airplane landing at this moment on a remote jungle airstrip. In it is a missionary whose heart is filled with the gospel of Christ. It is not too much of a stretch to think that the aluminum parts of that lightweight aircraft could have been handled by my father. One man doing one job touched by the Almighty. What an honor.

Because of this possibility, I deeply admire all types of labor. From those who string the wires through which electricity comes to our homes and lights our nights to the one who puts the switch in my truck so I can enjoy inspiring music, I so appreciate the network of laborers. May my son be numbered among those whose labors God honors because they honor God with the works of their hands.

Whatever you do, do your work heartily, as for the Lord rather than for men (Colossians 3:23).

Let your light shine before men in such a way that they may *see your good works, and glorify your Father who is in heaven* (Matthew 5:16, emphasis added).

4

Choosing the Right Hero

*Then David ran and stood over the Philistine and took
his sword and drew it out of its sheath and killed him,
and cut off his head with it. When the Philistines saw
that their champion was dead, they fled.*

1 SAMUEL 17:51

When the hero of the Philistines fell, an Israelite hero was
born. The young psalmist David was "the man." Yet only 36
chapters later he, too, took a fall when he sinned with Bathsheba. Is there any human that can fill the role of the perfect
hero? The answer was a resounding No!—*until Christ was born.*

I was born in 1950 in the great state of West Virginia.
Nestled in the state's southern mountain range was the town
of Chapmanville in Logan County. Though a small community by comparison to the big, modern metropolis of the cap-
ital city of Charleston, we were not deprived of the latest
technologies that were sweeping across the nation. One of
those wonders was the television.

As a kid, I can remember how excited we were to welcome our new "one-eyed family member" to our living room.

We were very eager to take in whatever could be sent to the tube via the airways, so much so that we were willing to even enjoy the "test lines" that the station would broadcast. For about 30 minutes before they actually signed on, especially on Saturday mornings, my sister and I would sit cross-legged on the floor with chin in hands and patiently stare at the TV while listening to a continuous, high-pitched tone that came through the little speaker.

Suddenly the sound would stop. That was the signal that a voice was about to announce the beginning of the broadcast day. We could hardly contain our joy as the images began to fill the screen in living black and white!

It didn't take too many weeks of viewing for our favorite shows to be established. Their scheduled airtime was fiercely anticipated, and social calendars were willingly altered to make sure we were in front of the set when they came on.

My favorite 30-minute adventure that kept me spellbound every seventh day was the first choice of a lot of my seven-year-old friends. Week after week we tuned in to this particular show, and often on the next day we would meet to reenact what we had seen. Our play times were devoted to pretending to be the character we had grown to love. In the privacy of our individual dreams, we *were* the man we saw on the screen—at least that was true for me.

The following portion of a song tells the tale of how dangerously effective the TV media was on our young, impressionable minds.

You Need Another Hero

Back in 1957
The man in red and blue
Could fly through the heavens

So…I tied a towel around my neck
It felt so good flowing down my back
I climbed out on the windowsill
That second story fall was very real
And when I came to, my daddy said to me

"You need another hero
Someone else you can follow
Who won't lead you astray wherever you go
You need another hero."[6]

I can't help but wonder how many grownup, American baby-boomer-"bubbas" would admit to doing something as silly as the kid in that lyric. Many of us whose hair is now either gray or graying probably have a special place in our hearts for the "man in red and blue." (For those rare few who may be in the dark regarding the mysterious flying man, let me put it this way: "It's a bird, it's a plane, *No!* It's Superman!")

Just saying that familiar phrase throws me back in time about 40 years. Of course, TV in those days was black and white. Had it not been for color pictures on things like cereal boxes and school lunch-pail lids, we wouldn't have known what color Superman's skintight outfit was. Even if we had never been informed of that detail, however, it would not have taken away from the incredible excitement that filled the screen each week. Just being able to view the caped hero's actions provided plenty of emotion for a seven year old to enjoy.

As far as my gullible mind was concerned, my hero was real. And so were the injuries that occurred when I tried to do what he did. But for some strange reason, the sprained ankles and jammed wrist joints didn't seem to faze me when my attempts to take flight went bad. I would simply retighten my towel, climb up on something high enough to jump off of, and try again.

It took a while for me to figure out why I couldn't sail through the air like he did. At first I assumed I didn't believe in him hard enough. I felt like I failed my hero. I couldn't see that in truth he had failed me. He never once looked into the camera, and said, "Steve, don't jump out of second-story windows and expect to fly. Don't try to stop bullets with your chest, even if your pajama top has a big "S" on the front. The things you see me do are merely illusions created by technology. Please don't try this at home!" Instead, without any warnings or disclaimers, I was led to believe his superhuman actions were factual and doable.

Thanks be to God, however, that I had a dad like the father in the previous lyric. While he understood how active the imagination of a child could be and allowed me the fun of being a kid, he never encouraged the kind of unbridled worship of fictitious characters that was developing in America's children.

Instead, he was careful to guide me to the truest of heroes whom he knew would not lead me astray. His name is Jesus Christ—the one who could do more than leap tall buildings with a single bound. He ascended bodily into heaven (Acts 2:32,33). He was more powerful than a locomotive. He defeated the forces of death, hell, and the grave (1 Corinthians 15:22). He could do far greater feats than look through walls. He was able to see through the wicked schemes of Satan and successfully resist the temptations that pounded Him in the wilderness for 40 days (Luke 4:1-13). It was this divine hero that my wise father pointed me to when I was a youngster. Dad wanted me to know Him, to believe in Him, and to embrace His supernatural abilities that were not generated by camera trickery. So...I did. And to this day I have not been disappointed (or injured) as a result of following Him!

I was bound and determined to teach my son that the real Savior of mankind was not born in Hollywood, but in Bethlehem.

Eventually, my turn came to be the dad who would guide a young son through the maze of this world's heroes. Incredibly, the same media that battled for the minds, hearts, and loyalties of youngsters 40 years ago is still grasping for them today. And Nathan saw the parade. From the driver of the "Knight Rider" car to the pilot of the "Air Wolf" helicopter, from the fast flying "Luke Skywalker" to the wall climbing "Spiderman," the would-be heroes kept coming. The competition for his affections was stiff, but I refused to give up. I was bound and determined to teach my son that the *real* Savior of mankind was not born in Hollywood, but in Bethlehem.

To deal with the "superhero syndrome," I found a great way to help Nathan understand the deceptive potential of the TV camera. We were traveling on a two-week tour and had a day off from our concerts. We checked into a hotel, but the kids were disappointed that the swimming pool was empty. But I got an idea.

Nathan was about six at the time. I appointed him the actor, I played the role of director, and Annie did the camera work. I instructed Nathan to run to the edge of the deep end of the empty pool and stop just long enough to turn around and wave at the camera, then dive in. The tension of the drama grew as Nathan moved toward the pool's edge, stopped and gave a happy-go-lucky wave, then proceeded to dive in. I was standing at the bottom, unseen by the camera's eye. When Nathan landed safely in my arms, I called to Annie, "Stop the camera and hold perfectly still."

As his mama waited motionless I instructed Nathan to lay face down on the dry floor of the pool. To make it look as though he had splattered on the concrete I positioned his legs in a contorted fashion and told him to not move. I then stepped out of the scene and instructed Annie to restart the camera. On cue she slowly walked to the edge and then gradually panned down to show what appeared to be our son's lifeless body laying sprawled out at the bottom of the pool.

When we got the film back from the processor I could hardly wait to show the home movie. Sure enough, just as planned, it looked like Nathan had sadly plummeted to his death by mistakenly diving into the deep end of an empty pool. The lesson was successful. From then on, Nathan was "on to" Hollywood's high-dollar cinematic pranks. It was some of the best firsthand knowledge he ever received. But there was something more important for him to understand.

I wanted Nathan to get the message that except for Christ, everyone would fail him. These many years later, Nathan's wife, Stephanie, wrote a song that accurately confirms what needs to be said. There's volumes of truth in the chorus of Stephanie's lyric entitled "Hey, MacGyver!"

> Hey, MacGyver, I've got duct tape and a ball point pen
> Can you get me out of the mess that I'm tangled in

I have watched you so faithfully since the age of ten
But you're nowhere now[7]

The last line of this refrain says it all. Heroes like Mac-Gyver and the rest of the weekly one-hour wonders do not stand the test of time. Christ alone has endured.

Fathers, too, are on the list of those who ultimately disappoint sons. As much as I would have loved to be the perfect role model for Nathan, I had one major hindrance: I was human. And no human could fully meet the need my young son had for a flawless leader to follow. But I wasn't completely off the hook! Though I knew I could not claim the role of his ultimate hero, I also understood that in no way was I free to relax my efforts to be a good example. To the contrary, I felt an even greater pressure to pursue righteousness. The apostle Paul boldly said to the Corinthians: "Be imitators of me, just as I also am of Christ" (1 Corinthians 11:1). Taking my cue from the apostle's brave claim, I knew that to help my son recognize and appreciate Christ as his greatest hero, I would have to strive to be one of the dads who were willing to "be imitators of God, as beloved children" (Ephesians 5:1). Thankfully, I found that living a normal Christian life provided plenty of chances to reflect His character.

Displaying the nature of Christ as a "rescuer" conveniently came one winter night near our house in Tennessee. And it happened without my consciously thinking, "Ah ha! This is my chance to show my boy how to act like the Lord!" I had driven to our local discount mart to pick up a few things and, as I was leaving the huge parking lot, I noticed a motor home with an attached utility trailer parked on the far end. There was some fancy writing on the side of the trailer. Though I couldn't read it in the distance, I had a feeling it was a vehicle used by a music group.

Someone was lying on the pavement underneath the unit obviously in "repair" mode. Having had my share of on-the-road, fix-it adventures, I headed to the motor home. Sure enough, I learned that the man was attempting to get the generator back into running order.

The weather was extremely frigid, and the temperature was dropping by the hour. The man had his family huddled in the cold, cavernous interior of the home on wheels. He thanked me for my concern and informed me there were plenty of blankets aboard their vehicle if they needed them. I wasn't convinced that their dashboard heat would suffice, and running the main engine all night also seemed hazardous.

Feeling empathy and sympathy for the shivering little family, I did something dangerous. Without first going to a phone and consulting with Annie, I asked the fellow to start up his rig and follow me to my residence. Within ten minutes we rolled up in front of our house. I went in and gave my family a fair warning that five complete strangers were about to enter. I explained their plight to Annie and, bless her heart, she accepted the challenge with an understanding smile. As it turned out, the group was a Christian singing family from Oklahoma. They spent the night in our home, and the next day some professional help was enlisted for the generator repair. They were soon on their way.

I was privileged to rescue some suffering saints. As they filed into our warm house, it didn't dawn on me that Nathan was watching. I was simply being faithful to the Lord's call to meet a need. One of the unexpected benefits of the obedience was that Nathan's observance of a good deed done helped him see the spirit of Christ.

The years have yielded other moments when I consciously and unconsciously tried to be a good example.

Standing with me as I picketed in front of an abortion clinic and taking the verbal abuse from the "pro-death" supporters, all for the sake of the unborn, is one example. Another attempt took place when he saw me stand firm and challenge a convenience store owner's unwise decision to sell pornography. To be honest, my ability to maintain composure in the midst of these kinds of confrontations left me looking like a scared Barney Fife. But in spite of my nervous demeanor, I obeyed the Lord. And my son watched a weak human make an attempt to be strong like his Eternal Hero.

Nathan is now nearing his mid-twenties, and I'm confident he understands that to see the very greatest of champions he must keep looking heavenward to Christ. All others, no matter how celebrated, will fall short of top billing. Recently, something happened in the world of sports that once again illustrated this truth. It left the two of us, along with my dad, shocked to the very core of our beings.

For quite some time the three of us have shared an ongoing and growing interest in the world of NASCAR auto racing. We've been to several professional races together, and Nathan and I have even been privileged (or "crazy," as Annie puts it) to sit behind the wheel of an official-sized, full-powered race car and drive well over 100 MPH around the Charlotte Speedway in North Carolina. With those few minutes of unbelievably exciting, in-car, firsthand experience, our appreciation for the incredible physical and mental abilities of the pro drivers skyrocketed.

One of our favorite personalities we followed on the racing circuit was Dale Earnhardt. We watched in horror as he reached the end of the race of life on the last lap of the 2001 Daytona 500. "The Intimidator," as he was known, had captured our attention from the very beginning. As far as we were concerned, the way anyone counted to four, at least in our neck of the woods, was: "1...2...Earnhardt...4."

He was the best of the best. When it came to racing, he was on the "pit stop pedestal." But when he died, the entire nation, not just racing fans, mourned. People from all walks of American life found themselves caught up in the sadness. I couldn't help but wonder why there was such an intense outpouring of sympathy among so many. As I thought about it, I realized that Dale Earnhardt's death came at a unique time in American history. I believed, as did others, that we as a nation had just finished eight years of reckless moral leadership. An untold number of questionable activities by President Bill Clinton were swept under the rug. Consequently, something had been absent far too long in America—a true hero. It's as if the citizens, whose sense of honor was still intact, were ready to collectively esteem someone—anyone—who was great.

Humans are far too fragile to be worshiped. We were not designed for it.

That's when Dale Earnhardt hit the wall. He was a man with a single, amazing skill. With merely an eighth-grade education, he built a multimillion-dollar racing empire. More importantly, he lived his life relatively free of scandals. To my knowledge, his only negative was that he tapped more bumpers on the race track than anyone else. His leadership in the industry ended in the fourth and final turn of the Super Bowl of races. This 49-year-old athlete, and father of the driver of the second-place car just ahead of him on the track that day, suddenly left our presence. We were absolutely and completely stunned. How could someone as nice and as giving as Dale leave so abruptly?

The sad days that followed provided one more opportunity for Nathan to be reminded of what I so desperately wanted him to know. Humans are far too fragile to be worshiped. We were not designed for it. And, furthermore, God will not be replaced. In fact, we have a biblical precedent that warns us that we should be very careful to not hold on to adulation but to pass the glory on to the Lord. In Acts 12, Herod the king did not refuse the praise of the people. Instead, after he had spoken to the throngs, he accepted their adulation when they cried, "The voice of a god and not of a man!" Verse 23 is a sobering commentary on what can happen when a human decides to bask in the glow of being worshiped: "And immediately an angel of the Lord struck him because he did not give God the glory, and he was eaten by worms and died."

Such is the eventual demise of all men and women who would allow themselves to be exalted as heroes without using that status to lift up the name of Christ. Here's a good rule to keep in mind when choosing an earthly example to follow: When the spotlight falls on a person and he or she is not found agreeing with John 3:30, "He must increase, but I must decrease," then that person is disqualified as someone worthy to imitate.

Remember when the apostle Paul encouraged others to imitate him? He could do this because he was careful to point them to the Holy One who had made the difference in his life. Jesus is our ultimate example. I want my son to know that no one rivals the eternally pure quality of the Lord Jesus. Unlike a fiction character, Jesus will never lead us to unwittingly jump out of a second-story window. He will never lose control and hit the wall. He will never leave us hopeless. The search for absolute greatness ends with Him. "If you trust Christ, you don't need another hero!"

5

First Comes Love…

"Having girded your loins with truth…" It is no mistake that in Ephesians 6:14, the first piece of the "full armor of God" that man is directed to place on himself involves the area of his reproductive organ. Satan, the enemy of our souls, knows very well where a man's first weakness may be. It's as though the evil one knows if he can strike us in that area, he'll defeat us for sure.

I'll never forget the popular gift book I saw on the shelf at our local bookstore. The cover was attractive and the title was even more appealing: *What Men Know About Women*. When I picked it up and opened it, I discovered that the pages were completely blank from cover to cover. And every unwritten word was true!

Knowing from personal experience that guys can indeed be clueless when it comes to understanding the opposite sex, I looked with great concern at my young son when he was in his preadolescent years. I was aware that the day would eventually come when deep in his youthful body a biological valve would mysteriously open and the first drop of a future river of hormones would be released into his system. At that moment he would realize that girls, as one man said, "are not just soft boys." Thus would begin one of the greatest and most important challenges he would ever face—to understand, appreciate, and more importantly, to rightly relate to the marvelous creation called woman.

The sobering part of having a son who would start to "notice" girls was that if I was not careful to be the one to write on those blank pages in his mind, someone else would. Fearing that others, especially his peers, might inscribe errant information that would steer his urges in the wrong direction, I determined to step in and beat them to the punch.

When Nathan was at the tender age of ten years old, I took the first step in alerting him to the fact that a "wild beast" would soon awaken in him. To do so I decided to use a tried-and-true method that males often enlist to create an environment for sharing deeply from the soul. I planned an adventure! It seems that the "distraction of action" helps men communicate better. It's as if a fellow's mouth moves much easier as long as his hands, feet, and eyes are in motion. Their movements work like a "conversation pump."

I was convinced that the excitement was more than sufficient to cushion the impact of the shocking "facts of life" that my son's mind was going to experience.

As it turned out, God provided the perfect activity. It was an NBA playoff game in Atlanta between the Hawks and the Chicago Bulls (with Michael Jordan). But that's not all. To secure a hard to find ticket, I called the Fellowship of Christian Athletes office in Georgia to enlist their help and discovered the director was an acquaintance who used to live in Nashville. I told him of my plans to have "the talk" with Nathan and that I was looking for something exciting to surround it. Little did I know that an incredible thing would happen. Knowing our family performed Christian music, he invited Nathan and me to provide the devotion at the pregame chapel service. Many of the famous players would be there, and we would be guests in the locker rooms. *Unbelievable!* We couldn't wait for the day to come when we would head south. I was convinced that the excitement was more than sufficient to cushion the impact of the shocking "facts of life" that my son's mind was going to experience.

It was during the four-hour drive to Atlanta that I delivered the bulk of the information I wanted him to hear. Fortunately, I had some help. I will be forever grateful for the audiotape version of Dr. James Dobson's book *Preparing for Adolescence*. I told Nathan that "The Doctor" had put into better words the things I wanted to say. I also informed him that he could stop the tapes at any point to discuss the subjects.

The trip to Atlanta was unforgettable. After several stops and starts of the tapes, along with discussions of the contents, Nathan got an earful and my emotions were drained. Though the two of us felt a great joy as a result of having had such an honest time of listening and conversing, there was a certain sadness that filled my heart. When we left Nashville, my son was a little, innocent, uninformed boy. When we got to the hotel that evening he had in his mental possession some very grownup information. I knew he would never be the same.

Because he was now privy to some things that others his age might not have yet heard, I did something to help him feel responsible with it. In the room were two wrapped plastic drinking cups. I opened one and asked Nathan to go to the sink and fill it to the very brim with water. I stood on the far side of the room and said, "Now, walk toward me at your regular pace." As he did, a good bit of the water spilled out and fell to the carpet.

Then I repeated the instructions. When he was ready to walk across the room again I stopped him and said, "This time, I want you to come to me with that cup of water and not spill a drop. That means you have to take each step very carefully." He slowly worked his way to me, and I congratulated him for a cup that was still full. Then I said, "Son, that cup is like your heart. Today, it has been filled with some of the most important things you'll ever hear. However, it would not be wise to spill it onto your friends. They may not be ready to hear it. Plus, their dads may want to be present when they do. That's why you must walk as carefully with the information you've been given as you did the second time you carried that cup of water across the room. It is your responsibility to not spill a drop. I know you'll do as well." And he did. He's a fine one!

As the day ended, I thought of how differently my dad had handled the same conversation with me. His method was a lot simpler and much less expensive, yet just as effective. He delivered his version of "the talk" the day I left for college. As the car was about to back out of the driveway he leaned into the window, looked at me with an expression that only men can understand, and said, "Son, keep your zipper up!" I knew exactly what he was saying...and I had a bladder problem for years. (Just kidding!) Seriously, what more could be said? What better advice could be given? He went straight to the bottom line.

Basically, my dad's simple order was similar to what God demanded of Cain when he was fighting his terribly bad attitude of jealousy against his brother, Abel. God sternly said, "Sin is crouching at the door; and its desire is for you, but you must master it" (Genesis 4:7). My dad's short command was long on truth. It implied the same principle that Cain had heard. "Steve, you take charge of your zipper. Don't let the devil win." I bless my dad for saying so much with so few words.

Nathan and I returned home from Atlanta and time went on. As he passed through his eleventh and twelfth birthdays, we didn't say too much about girls and sex other than an occasional inquiry about how he was doing with his "awakening." We did have a few brief conversations that seemed necessary, but always awkward. For the most part, I simply observed him closely and prayed a lot that the sacred information I had given him when he was ten would be carefully guarded by the warriors of the Lord as promised in Psalm 91:11: "For He will give His angels charge concerning you, to guard you in all your ways."

When his thirteenth birthday came I sensed that my son's battle with his hormones was becoming very real and regular. How did I know? Was it a supernatural revelation that woke me one night to tell me my boy was struggling with the invasion of his manhood? Of course not. I knew he was at war with his hormones because I was once his age. I vividly remember my struggle. It was intense and unrelenting.

How could I ever forget, for example, the unquenchable thirst for my first kiss? My desire to experience pressing my lips on that of a girl's drove me to do something that is filed away in my heart under the "most embarrassing moments" category. Her name was _____ . (Did you really think I would reveal such information? She might read this!) We were both close to our thirteenth birthdays, and we were standing under the light of an exposed 60-watt bulb on the small concrete porch of her house. It was a frigid December night in West Virginia and the 15-degree temperature made us shuffle our feet in order to stay warm. We made small talk and shivered.

I knew what I wanted to do, and I think she knew as well. Furthermore, I assumed she wanted to do what I wanted to do and I was hoping she did. There was a strange and wonderful tension that grew between us as we hem-hawed and rocked back and forth on our numbing feet. I decided, before we both froze to death, it was time to make my move. I cocked my head sideways, just like I had seen them do on TV, and moved in closer to her face. She stopped moving. I was motionless as we looked into each other's eyes. It was a classic romantic moment for two curious adolescents. A spark was about to fly. Then something dreadfully disturbing caught my eye.

Under the light I got a glimpse of a substance that made me question my attempt to get that first kiss. The unbelievable cold had caused "it" to gather in that indention in the face that runs from the bottom center of the nose to the top of the upper lip. That little fleshly ditch had filled with a neon green stream. My stomach flipped over about three times—and it wasn't love that did it. I immediately assessed the situation and realized I was in a serious dilemma. If I backed off I might hurt her feelings. If I went through with my plan, I might die. What to do?

I opted to follow through but not linger long like they did on the television shows. A quick connect and I'd be out of there, perhaps with my reputation undamaged. So I closed my eyes and pressed in. When my face touched hers I slid off her mouth onto the side of her face and nearly banged my head on the aluminum storm door behind her head. I snapped my head back instantly and when I was about five inches from her face I realized, to our horror, we were still connected. The string of green hung for a moment between us like a skipping rope. Thankfully, when it broke it fell her way. I said a quick goodbye and ran off the little porch and didn't stop until I reached the bathroom of my house.

I want my son to know that God has a time line for enjoying the "full beauty" of a woman.

The mixture of feelings that followed me home that night are still with me today. On one lip, I was excited to have gotten my first smooch. But on the other, it's snot a memory of romance that I want to cling to. It was definitely not the way I thought the "unquenchable thirst" for a first kiss would be satisfied.

While this true story reveals my anxiousness to acquire a taste of carnal knowledge, it represents a mere ember from the "fire of desire" that was racing through my young heart. Knowing the same flames would reach the field of my son's mind, I wanted to add one other piece of information about girls to what he had learned on our way to Atlanta. I knew the best source for that knowledge was found in the Scriptures. And I believed that if he carried this truth from God's Word through his dating years, he had a better chance of reaching the other end of the "girl gauntlet" with his good morals intact. That truth?

Being attracted to the form of the female is as natural as breathing. Appreciating the fact that females are different from males is a God-given gift to men. Genesis 2:22 reports that God escorted His new creation to the first man, Adam. Suddenly there Eve stood in all of her unclothed glory. Adam, to that point, had never seen a woman. As he looked at her, did God rebuke him? Absolutely not. He allowed Adam to ponder her presence.

After an amount of time, Adam finally spoke. "This is now bone of my bones, and flesh of my flesh; she shall be called Woman, because she was taken out of Man." (Some guys believe Adam's reaction to seeing Eve was, "Whoa! Man!" Thus, wo-man...woman!)

God did not scold Adam for feasting his eyes on the Creator's glorious "riblet." That private moment between a man and a woman and their Maker was free of guilt and conflict. It appears that man was "wired" to find joy at the sight of a woman. Furthermore, God seemed pleased that Adam was so impressed with what he had seen.

Nathan needed to understand that the first meeting of a man's eyes and a woman's flesh was in a holy environment. It was for that reason that chapter 2 of Genesis could end with "and the man and his wife were both naked and were not ashamed." It wasn't until the craftiness of Satan enticed the two of them to disobey God that it was written, "Then the eyes of both of them were opened, and they knew that they were naked; and they sewed fig leaves together and made themselves loin coverings" (Genesis 3:7). And in verse 10,

"And [Adam] said, 'I heard the sound of You [God] in the garden, and I was afraid because I was naked; so I hid myself.'"

In order for my son to understand his fallen, sinful nature and that he must do battle against it—especially in regard to sexual behavior—he had to realize he is a descendant of Adam. One of the best evidences that Adam is in his blood is found in what he does every morning before he leaves the house. My son's Adamic nature is revealed when he chooses to put on clothes before going into public. There is a mysterious call in every human that begs us to cover ourselves and not show up "in the buff" when we go outside. To cover our nakedness is an ancient impulse time has not erased. (There are those who would deny this, but to reject the imprint of shame placed in our hearts on the day Adam and Eve first sinned is to say God has no place in our lives. Nudist colonies, sunny beaches, neighborhood swimming pools, and even concert stages are filled with people who disregard God's standards for decency. Eventually they become so calloused that they lose their sensitivity to His Holy Spirit and give themselves over to sensuality for the practice of every kind of impurity [see Ephesians 4:19].)

Nathan must also be on guard against the people who want to exploit our God-given desires. The proliferation of pornography and related industries documents the moral decline in this country. The word "pornography" comes from the Greek word *porneo*, which, in the original language, is often interpreted as "harlot." My son needs to know that to allow a woman to draw him off the path of righteousness is to take the pathway to destruction. The following song lyric was written many years ago for Nathan to hear and remember. It is an adaptation of the Proverbs 7 warning about "the harlot."

List of Fools

I was standing at my window when I saw a young
  man
Walking late at night near her corner
He was old enough to be there but too young to
  understand
The sorrow he had found when he met her
She was dressed like a harlot, she had evil on her mind
Not looking for a lover, just a victim
And with her words she flattered him and it scattered
  his good sense
And I knew that boy was caught when she kissed him

And tonight she will add him to her long list of fools
And leave him to suffer in his wounds
Her pleasure for a moment will give him years of pain
To know his name is on a harlot's list of fools

Oh you young men, won't you listen to some wisdom
Don't you get caught in her ways
'Cause her house is on the highway that'll lead you to
  your grave
Don't let her take you astray

'Cause if you do she'll just add you to her long list of
  fools
And leave you to suffer in your wounds
Her pleasure for a moment will give you years of pain
To know your name is on a harlot's list of fools.[8]

Oh, how I long for my son's name to never be found on
that sad list. I know it will be very difficult for him to avoid,
especially because the harlot and what she represents is no
longer available only on side streets. Today, she walks the
streets of technology. Now, in the privacy of a room in his

house, a man can flip a switch, push an "on" button, or click on a computer mouse and suddenly he is in her chambers. The risk of embarrassment and being accountable to other humans for his actions is gone. In an instant, without stepping foot on the street, he is on his way to the grave of her presence. Nathan and I have discussed the fact that adultery with a "virtual harlot" is just as sinful as the act done in the flesh. Proverbs 6:25 and Matthew 5:28 are clear warnings that fornication is a serious sin even if done mentally: "Do not desire her [the harlot] beauty in your heart"; "everyone who looks at a woman with lust for her has already committed adultery with her in his heart."

I also pray that he will understand that marriage is not a cure for lust.

God has an order, or time line, for enjoying the beauty of a woman. For sure, the initial step is not the sexual relationship. The beginning point is found in a phrase from an old, familiar schoolyard rhyme, and it is more profound than one may realize: "first comes love..."

Having love be the starting place was God's idea. He wants men to first embrace women as His gift to us: "For indeed man was not created for the woman's sake, but woman for the man's sake" (1 Corinthians 11:9). (A Tennessee paraphrase that might make it easier for "bubba" to understand is: "You ain't God's gift to women!")

First Peter 3:7 refers to the woman as a "weaker vessel" (KJV). As one gentleman suggested, this is a beautiful way of saying she's a fine work of art, such as a priceless Tiffany lamp or a centuries old Stradivari violin. In the same way he would cherish a work of brilliance like these, a man must protect the value of a woman. To reduce her form to a self-serving, self-gratifying source to feed a sexual appetite is far from pleasing to God, her Maker.

I want Nathan to know that he must strive to find favor with the Lord when it comes to rightly treating a woman and preserving a godly love for her. To do so, he must be willing to "flee from youthful lust" (2 Timothy 2:22). He must be ready to turn his tail and run. None of us looks with disgust at Joseph who fled from the presence of Potiphar's pretty wife in Genesis 39:12. Instead, most of us consider young Joseph's actions as incredibly smart, even though he paid the price of going to prison to maintain his righteousness. Only a fool would say, "Joseph missed his big chance!"

I also pray that my son will understand that marriage is not a cure for lust. The battle to maintain morally pure thoughts about a woman will continue into his later years, assuming he experiences no major medical problems.

Jerry Jenkins, coauthor of the well-known *Left Behind* series, offered a life-changing insight about 2 Timothy 2:22. He noted that the word "youthful" in the passage certainly applies to the need for teens to corral their sexual emotions, but it also reveals that the struggle to maintain purity will be "youthfully intense" throughout life.

My 96-year-old grandfather was proof that Jerry's comment was true. After outliving two women, my granddad was looking for his third wife when he died. The last thing to expire when he passed away was his hormones. And I'm his grandson!

Because I am Nathan's "old man" (remember chapter 1?), I know what he's going through to preserve purity in his heart because I, too, am weak. But, I have learned an important lesson from 2 Corinthians 12:9: [The Lord said,] "My grace is sufficient for you, for power is perfected in weakness." I want Nathan to know that whenever the temptation comes to destroy true love by enjoying sex outside of the protective bonds of marriage, he can cry out to God, *"I am weak!"* The moment he bravely makes this wise confession, something divinely wonderful happens. The admission of weakness turns that frailty into a container, into which God pours His strength. With the Lord's power filling his heart, my son can overcome the enemy's enticements.

Is there hope for a young man who has forfeited his purity by partaking in premarital sex? Certainly! God has not abandoned the person who has yielded to temptation. The following song was written to young ladies and young gents who have failed in this area. It reminds them of the hope found in the forgiving nature of our Father in heaven.

The Treasure

Girls, don't give your treasure away
It's for the man somewhere in time
   who is willing to wait
Until the day he can call you by his name
So girls, don't give his treasure away

But if you've done it
And you wonder
What you should do
Well, just remember
Go to Jesus
And He'll make you brand-new

And when He restores the treasure
To its original state
Until the right time,
Don't give it away

And young men
I know it's very hard to see
That just beyond the way
    you feel
Is the man you want to be
So keep it pure
For the woman who waits
And boys, don't give your
    treasure away

But if you've done it
And you wonder
What you should do
Just remember
Go to Jesus
And He'll make you brand-new
And when He restores
    the treasure
To its original state
Until the right time
Don't give it away[9]

This lyric has its roots in 2 Corinthians 5:17, which joyfully announces, "Therefore if anyone is in Christ, he is a new creature; the old things passed away; behold, new things have come." While virginity can never be restored once it is lost, certainly the pureness of the heart is regained when a life is given to Christ and experiences the forgiveness of sin. And, without a doubt, the level of purity God restores in a heart is a priceless treasure that can be offered without reservation to the person's future spouse.

For the son who finds that one of his greatest challenges to keeping his virginity comes from his peers who mock him for his innocence, I offer this story.

> A young college-aged man had entered school with a victorious record in regards to "keeping himself" for a future wife. His dormmates found out he was inexperienced and began to badger him mercilessly. One day the young man had taken enough harassment and turned to his dormies, and said, "Look, guys, I can join your club anytime I want to. But you can never join mine!" The pestering ceased. What a slice of brilliance God had given the young fellow.

To sum up, I want Nathan to know that if I have written nothing else on the pages of his personal copy of *What Men Know About Women,* I at least hope the following words will be found: "First comes love..."

6

Then Comes Marriage...

Husbands, love your wives, just as Christ also loved the
church and gave Himself up for her.

EPHESIANS 5:25

Getting married and getting "saved" are a little alike. Not much is known about either path before the journey begins.

Walking with Christ has been exceedingly and abundantly joyful. Even the hard lessons that had to be learned have been utterly rewarding. As for traveling the trail of life with my wife, Annie, I can say the same has been true! I want my son to know that the day he allows the two roads to join—his walk with the Lord and his life with his wife—then the truest of bliss is his.

One of the most sobering thoughts I can recall came to me a few months before our daughter's wedding. Annie and I were considering which person or pastor would be the best to provide premarital counseling for Heidi and her fiancé, Emmitt. As we pondered the choices, it suddenly occurred to me: *She's been in premarital counseling for 20 years!* My knees weakened and the sweat beads formed on my wrinkled and hairless forehead.

Since our children were old enough to breathe, they've been watching their mom and dad in the drama of marriage. It dawned on me that the kind of spouses they will become would be directly related to the kind of teachers Annie and I have been. The classroom where our kids have been learning about the skills of matrimony have been occupied nonstop for more than 7000 days. So, in reality, it's not *if* they learned anything, it is *what* they learned. This fact makes any parent cringe. All Annie and I could do was hope we had done some things well enough for our children's lives would benefit to some degree.

Heidi's November wedding came so quickly that it made my head and heart (and wallet) spin in disbelief. It was a beautiful event and worth every penny I will never see again. But the reprieve from spending our energies was brief. Before that unforgettable day had ended, our son had proposed to his girlfriend. (For almost three hours I wasn't writing checks! It was a good moment of rest.) Annie and I slid out of one emotional roller coaster and climbed right back into another. But it's quite fine with us. Our daughter-in-law is a welcomed addition to our lives. In fact, we have prayed for her arrival for years. The prayer was, "Oh, God, give Nathan the girl of *our* dreams." And He did!

In the time that remained prior to our family's second wedding in 11 months, I had plenty of opportunity to think about what helpful things I might say to my son. Knowing that my only qualification to be any kind of premarital counselor to him was found in the fact that I have been married to his mother for more than a quarter of a century, I set out to find a memorable way to deliver my limited knowledge. Thankfully, a great idea came from my sweet wife.

Since thousands of volumes have already been written about a husband's responsibility to his wife (and Nathan would do well to read some of them), I accepted Annie's suggestion to reduce my thoughts into the convenient space of an acrostic. Using the word "marriage" as a guide, what follows are some things I want my son to know about "becoming one with a woman." In no way does it exhaust all I wish for him to know—or all he needs to know—but it does touch the foremost issues that might be of some help to him.

M
Maximize Her Needs; Minimize Her Faults

With high hopes that a girl will be convinced that her affections can be safely entrusted into his care, a boy can display some amazing skills with the "emphasize her needs, overlook her faults" principle. For example, an unbetrothed fellow will sit at the table where the damsel of his dreams has prepared some tasty morsels. He picks up a biscuit made by the lovely hands of this delightful maiden. As he squeezes it to break it open so that he might butter it, he discovers that the item he has in his hands is not bread—it's a stone! It could have been used in the sling of David to bring down the giant Goliath. Knowing that Goliath's skull would collapse under such hardness, the boy has no doubt that his teeth would never be the same. Yet he understands that maximizing her needs and minimizing her faults must be the rule of the conquest. So, with a willingness to sacrifice his grinders, he bites into the biscuit. Afraid to smile for fear of revealing the possible new gaps in his dentures, he crunches, all the while offering an approving expression. She smiles.

Then his love sits down to eat with him. When she puts the spoon to her mouth he finds joy in the sight of her red lips, which he thinks are so beautiful and that he longs to kiss. However, what happens next serves to test his resolve concerning his pursuit of her love. When she starts chewing, the noises she makes rivals that of an entire battle with swords and cannons. For a moment he mentally grimaces, but then remembers, *maximize her needs; minimize her faults.* So he remains silent while she chomps away. With a willing resolve to ignore her odd trait, he presses on until at last, one day she lets him win the love pursuit. Finally the wedding vows are exchanged.

The years of matrimony go on and the two are living in bliss…until…one too many of his teeth have suffered her baking and suddenly her ear-damaging chomps get the best of his good nature. Somewhere along the way, there comes a reversal of the premarital attitude that had served him so well. He begins to maximize her faults and minimize her needs. When this happens, things get really tense. The affections the woman confidently placed in his hands are threatened. His patience with her kitchen and table habits, as well as all the other things that were once lovely but now barely tolerable, is wearing thin. What can the young lover do?

———

I unashamedly confess that I would be a complete, worthless slob without my wife. And, in a strange way, it comforts me to admit it.

———

This is what I want my son to know. First of all, the description of the two lovers is not that of his parents. Granted, Annie and I have had our bouts with some things that were ignored during the dating days, but we have learned how to deal with them. As a husband, I have come to understand that what was an instrument of *conquering* before the marriage vows must become the instrument of *keeping* afterward. If this metamorphosis does not take place in a man's heart, the potential for wounded feelings is far too great.

While there very well may be some character improvements that one mate can help the other accomplish, this must be done with great wisdom and gentleness. The high goal of a man lovingly accepting the imperfections of a woman while focusing on her deepest needs can be obtained if he knows Christ. That *keeping* tool can be found in Philippians 2:3,4:

> Do nothing from selfishness or empty conceit, but with humility of mind regard one another as more important than yourselves; do not merely look out for your own personal interests, but also for the interests of others.

And just as Jesus gave His life for us, so should the husband do as stated in Ephesians 5:25: "Husbands, love your wives, just as Christ also loved the church and gave Himself up for her." In Christ alone is found the epitome of a good husband.

As husband and wife, Annie and I have come to grips with certain things about each other that have the potential to put bad notes in our rhapsody of love. For example, we don't think alike on a plethora of issues. Though this is true, we have decided not to let our differences create a wedge between us. Just like chili would be bland without the spices, so would a marriage be without differences. Conceding to this attitude has served me well as a husband. The fact is, one has to yield to the other's uniqueness from time to time. The following song Annie and I sing as a duet lists several of the things we disagree about even to this day; yet, we remain the best of friends.

I want my son to know that if he will see his wife's needs as more important than his own, he can have the same joy.

Incompatibility

Steve: I like a little mayo
Annie: Mustard is my thing
Steve: Make my bread as white as cotton
Annie: I'll have wheat with seven grains;
    And a little candle glowing when we eat
    is what I like
Steve: I need to see what I'm consuming
    So please turn on the lights
Annie: I go to bed before the news
Steve: I'm still awake at 2 A.M.
Annie: I'm up before the chickens
Steve: If I can I'm sleeping in;
    I like wearing hunting clothes
Annie: I like hunting clothes to wear;
    I'll always ask directions
Steve: I'll find my own way there

chorus—Steve and Annie
We've got incompatibility
Everywhere we turn
But still we stay together
'Cause there's a lesson we have learned
That if this man and woman
Were in every way the same
One of us would not be needed
And wouldn't that be a shame

Annie: I like a walk in the park
Steve: I would rather run;
How far can we go on empty
Annie: I've never seen as fun

Steve: I like talking with my buddies
   When we're teeing off at ten
Annie: My greens and conversation
   Are a salad bar with friends
Annie: My feet are like December
Steve: Mine are like July
Annie: While I'm piling on the blankets
Steve: I lay there and fry
Annie: I married Ebenezer Scrooge
Steve: I married Mrs. Claus
Annie: While I'm watching *Casablanca*
Steve: I'd rather be watching Tennessee
   football

chorus—Steve and Annie
We've got incompatibility
Everywhere we turn
But still we stay together
'Cause there's a lesson we have learned
That if this man and woman
Were in every way the same
One of us would not be needed
And wouldn't that be a shame.[10]

A
Admit Your Need for Her

There seems to be something spiritually therapeutic that happens in a man's heart when he honestly admits he needs a woman. This could be true because deep in the recesses of his spirit, he knows he is agreeing with a declaration God made long, long ago in the Garden of Eden. Even though Adam was living in a perfect state with no disease, no death, no war, and no mosquitoes (hopefully), God said, "It is not good for the man to be alone; I will make him a helper suitable for him" (Genesis 2:18). This was the first time, by the way, that God said the words, "It is not good." How right He was! I unashamedly confess that I would be a complete, worthless slob without my wife. And, in a strange way, it comforts me to admit it.

I want Nathan to know that he comes from a long line of men who needed women in their lives. His Grandfather Williamson, Annie's dad, is a prime example. The story is told that on the day his fifth child was born he was out in the fields working. While he labored in the corn, his pregnant wife went into labor and was taken to the hospital. When he heard the news, he hurried home to get cleaned up and go to join her there. Unfortunately, one little detail had been overlooked by his wife, who had suddenly been preoccupied with birth pangs.

Normally, she laid out the clothes she wanted him to wear whenever the two of them went into public. The reason for this kind act was twofold. One, she was happy with how he looked. And two, he didn't have to think too much. They were both completely satisfied with this arrangement. However, when he was left alone to dress himself, something went terribly wrong. Grandfather Williamson showed up at the hospital wearing one of his wife's white blouses. When she saw what he had done, she declared, "No one should be that helpless!" Sylvia had definitely married a man who needed a woman.

I want Nathan to know that he, too, will do well to admit his need. Agreeing with God is a smart thing to do!

R
Rule over Your Tongue

This may very well be the toughest challenge a man can face. If mastering the words (including their tone) is not accomplished, he stands the chance of causing harm instead of harmony in his marriage. He cannot constantly use his tongue like a sword and uncontrollably jab with it, withdraw it, and *then* repent for offending. That kind of repeated abuse will ultimately result in the death of a woman's affections. Instead, he must be in charge of his tongue the moment a thought or a feeling tries to force its way out of his mouth.

In order to appreciate this need, it would be wise for all men to read, absorb, and live by James 3:2-10:

> For we all stumble in many ways. If anyone does not stumble in what he says, he is a perfect man, able to bridle the whole body as well. Now if we put the bits into the horses' mouths so that they will obey us, we direct their entire body as well.

> Look at the ships also, though they are so great and are driven by strong winds, are still directed by a very small rudder wherever the inclination of the pilot desires.

> So also the tongue is a small part of the body, and yet it boasts of great things. See how great a forest is set aflame by such a small fire! And the tongue is a fire, the very world of iniquity; the tongue is set among our members as that which defiles the entire body, and sets on fire the course of our life, and is set on fire by hell. For every species of beasts and birds, of reptiles and creatures of the sea, is tamed and has been tamed by the human race. But no one can tame the tongue; it is a restless evil and full of deadly poison. With it we bless our Lord and Father, and with it we curse men, who have been made in the likeness of God; from the same mouth come both blessing and cursing. My brethren, these things ought not to be this way.

If a husband heeds this advice, his marriage can experience levels of contentment unknown by far too many couples.

In all of his conquering, a man must fight daily to win the battle over the tongue. He must never give up until the day it rests quietly in the grave. To fail to engage in this battle will eventually disqualify him as a good lover. And what man would ever want that sad consequence!

How can I help Nathan win this war? The best information I can give him is found in Matthew 12:34: "For the mouth speaks out of that which fills the heart." Humans are like tubes of toothpaste. Sooner or later we get squeezed by the pressures of life. When this happens, whatever is in us comes out. Another illustration is found in an interesting event that takes place in West Virginia. Perhaps this unusual occurrence can be documented from other areas of the country, but as far as I know it is unique to the "Mountaineer State." During the summer there are "Ramp Festivals" in the hills. Ramps are a wild onion. Their potency makes garlic smell like the fragrance of a hyacinth. The most important thing to remember about the ramp, though, is that the smell is most putrid when it comes through the skin after eating them.

Served with ham and other country-type victuals, the ramps are consumed by the mountain masses. If everyone partakes, the nemesis that the rank can be to the nostrils is lessened significantly. However, if a person refrains from the veggie, he will pay for it when he gets in a crowd of folks whose bellies are full of them. As the warm days linger after the ramp dinner has been enjoyed, so does the aroma. It is especially pronounced when a person sweats. Whether he wants to or not, he reveals where he has been and what he's been eating.

The same is true when it comes to that which exudes from the heart by way of the tongue. When the "heat" is on, whatever a person has been taking in will come out. Does it smell sweet to the hearts of those around or could the aroma bring a runaway train to a screeching halt? A husband who has been consuming the Word of God will not offend his mate when the pressures of life force him to say something.

With this truth in mind, the very best thing I can suggest for my son to do is to fill his heart with the Scriptures. In those times when his tongue is called upon to report the contents of his soul, he will speak blessings instead of curses. There's not a woman alive who wouldn't appreciate being washed by the pure water of her husband's sanctified words that are rooted in the Scriptures (see Ephesians 5:26).

R
Resist the Tendency to Control Her

While it is normal for a man to embrace his role as protector of his wife, some men carry this responsibility to a dangerous extreme. I want my son to understand that his job as a husband is not to be a "dad" to his wife, but to be *a partner with her.*

There are two instances when I learned that it would be both inappropriate and undeserved to try to control my wife. The first one involves money. When archery deer season was nearing, I went to the local bow shop and ordered a dozen of the best arrows they offered. When I brought them home, Annie was working in the yard. I went to the garage and got my bow and my bucket of target arrows and carried them to the area of our backyard that I had turned into a small shooting range. The container held at least three dozen arrows. Then I went to the truck and got my new set and dropped them into the bucket. Annie observed the addition of the aluminum sticks to the already overflowing pail.

"Did you need that many new ones, dear?" she asked with a tone of doubt.

"Oh, yes, sweetheart! This gets me ready for the upcoming season." Of course, I didn't really need them but it felt good to know there were fresh, perfectly straight shafts to mount to my quiver.

"Uh hum!" Annie responded softly.

Now move ahead about two months. The Christmas season is approaching, and we have just finished a meal at a local country-style restaurant that has an attached craft shop. Annie made her way to the ornament rack. When I entered the cash register area to pay for our meal, I saw her carefully removing pretty little tree decorations, one by one. She was up to five or six when I stepped up and asked with a sigh, "What are you doing?"

Annie knew that I was very much aware of the untold number of ornaments she already had boxed in the attic. She also knew I was not keen on adding to the stack. However, when she answered my question, I knew better than to challenge her purchase. Why? Because her answer was, "I'm buying arrows." I walked away in silence, like any smart man would do.

What was the big deal? If I allowed myself to be like a lot of husbands I know, I would try to control her spending. However, because I trust Annie's financial sense and because I know it would be wrong if I bought things for myself and didn't expect her to do the same, then I would be guilty of being terribly unfair to her. How a husband handles this issue is a very readable gauge for how much he tries to control her.

The other instance when I knew I could not allow myself to dominate Annie involved her driving alone to West Virginia. When the health of Annie's parents began to fail, she intensely sensed the need to often drive the 450 miles to their home to assist her siblings in caring for their mother and father. I couldn't always make the trip with her, so she frequently made the journey without me. One evening, while having dinner with some friends, the hour was getting late and as we said our goodbyes Annie announced that she would be driving alone to West Virginia the next day. The host husband noticeably bristled and asked me with a scolding tone, "Are you going to let her drive all that way without you?"

Though I would have preferred to go along for the drive and even be behind the wheel, my response was a confident, "Sure!" He proceeded to rake me over the coals for not planning to accompany Annie on such a long trip. I felt quite parented by his rebuke but responded with, "Listen, my friend, first of all, if you want to try to stop her from going, be my guest! But Annie is a grown woman and fully capable of taking care of herself. If I didn't think she could, I would certainly have my foot on the gas pedal tomorrow." At that point his wife offered a silent but telltale grin as she stared at her husband. Annie smiled too as she heard me brag about her ability to take on the task of covering so many miles without me.

What do I want Nathan to get out of these examples? While his wife's duty, as stated in Ephesians 5:22, is to be "subject" to her husband, the word in the original language does not imply that she is *involuntarily* placed under his authority. Instead, she *willingly* sets herself in that position. Therefore, a husband must respect her abilities and earn her trust in his leadership. In no way should he try to lord his headship role over her. To do so will inflict irreparable damage to their relationship.

I

Invest in Her Natural Gifts and Talents

One of the most exciting things about knowing Annie has been discovering the God-given gifts she possesses. When we met in 1963, I had no idea that inside the dairy farmer's daughter were some incredible abilities that would someday surface. It was around 1967, for example, that I learned how well she could sing. As I sat in the high school choir room and heard her deliver a beautiful solo, her voice was like a healing balm on a wounded soul. To this day it is still sweet to my ears.

It was not too many years later, in the midst of the confusion of the 1970s, that I found Annie's gift of wisdom. I was caught up in the socially rebellious spirit of the age and my "lostness" was evident in the songs I was writing. I invited Annie to my parents' house to listen to a tune I had recorded. It was a "Bob Dylanesque" song that was long in lyric but short on sense. When the tape reached the end, I turned the machine off and asked, "What do you think?" Without batting her pretty eyes, she answered, "That sounds like the product of a confused mind." Was I devastated? Absolutely not! Instead, I was swept off my feet. Right there in the basement of my parents' house I was standing next to a genius. She had seen right through my attempt to be someone I didn't need to be. Her insightful response is one of the many reasons I gleefully cleave to her today! My mama didn't raise no fool!

I want my son to willingly invest his energy in finding his wife's natural abilities and doing everything necessary to develop them, including spending his hard-earned dollars. I have happily purchased everything from Crock-Pots to computers to give my sweetheart the tools she needs to use her gifts. Ephesians 5:29 points out that "no one ever hated his own flesh, but nourishes and cherishes it." Annie and I are one flesh, so I don't mind treating her as I treat myself. It's the right thing to do. Besides, I was sure that every dollar I poured into her life would yield a hundredfold return in our marriage. *And I was right!* The cooking tools resulted in new "folds" in my waistline, and the computer has given birth to more than eight books. It has been money, time, and effort well spent.

A
Admit Your Mistakes

I know this is the second time the word "admit" appears in this acrostic, but as far as men are concerned, it's a verb that can never be overused. This is especially true when it comes to dealing with the fact that it's not *if* we are going to mess up, it's *when.*

I love the story about the husband who was looking in his closet one day and saw a cigar box on the shelf he had not noticed before. He pulled it down, opened it up, and was puzzled to find that inside were six eggs and $1500 in cash. He took it to his wife, and asked, "Honey, what is this?"

She responded with a startled, "Oh! You found it." She then went ahead and offered an explanation. "Well, since we married 23 years ago, each time you made a mistake I put an egg in that box." He thought to himself, *Wow! 23 years of marriage and only six mistakes. Man! Am I doing good or what?*

As he silently gloated about his fine history, he was curious to know more about the contents of the box. "Well, what about all this cash?"

She hesitantly answered, "Every time I got a dozen eggs I sold them...for 50 cents."

Needless to say, that fellow would have done well to have never found the box. But, in truth, his dilemma is common to most of us guys. I want my son to know that we all mess up at one time or another. The important thing is that we are willing to admit it when we do.

"Confess your sins to one another, and pray for one another so that you may be healed." While this admonition in James 5:16 is directed to the followers of Christ everywhere, it certainly applies to husbands and wives who care about the spiritual health of their marriages. And the husband should be the first to exemplify this attitude. Without it, a root of bitterness could spring up and cause trouble.

G
Go Often to the Lord in Prayer *with* Her

I want Nathan to know that prayer is a mighty weapon God has given to two people who are married. Praying together is a tremendous challenge for many husbands.

Matthew 18:19 is one of the most treasured passages in Annie's heart and mine: "Again I say to you, that if two of you agree on earth about anything that they may ask, it shall be done for them by My Father who is in heaven." Perhaps one of the reasons this promise is offered by Christ is that He knows how amazing it is when two people agree on anything! Since the tendency of human beings is to be sinfully selfish, when they come to God with a mutual goal it gets His attention.

I have seen the value of combined prayer in our own marriage. In fact, even before our wedding day God showed us His ability and desire to respond to our petitions. A few weeks before we were married, Sarah, the name we gave our 1950 Chevy because she was old and still productive, was sick unto death. Her transmission had failed and left us stranded on the highway. As we sat along the road, we held hands and agreed in prayer, asking God for a miracle. The petition went something like this: "Lord, I've never prayed for a car before...because up till now, I've driven Fords!

(Okay, I didn't include the part about Fords.) But Sarah is sick. Would You please touch her? We need Your grace."

God "healed" Sarah right before our very eyes! We had no one else to thank for the blessing of a fresh, working clutch. A few minutes earlier, when we pulled our ailing car off the road, we were just another young couple on a date. However, when we shot back onto the highway in our new, heavenly restored machine, we were a prayer team! Oh, what a difference God can make in two people's lives.

Though that experience was a one-time thing, God has certainly not been sleeping since. We have joyfully watched Him grant other petitions we have made—from miraculously bringing a loved one to a saving knowledge of His grace, to healing our sick children. We know from experience that prayer is effective.

I want Nathan to always be mindful that God cares about every facet of his marriage. I want him to know that he can take the hand of his mate and confidently approach God's throne if both of them individually and mutually believe in Christ and in the promise found in Hebrews 4:16: "Therefore let us draw near with confidence to the throne of grace, so that we may receive mercy and find grace to help in time of need."

E

Engage the Gears of Sex in the Right Order

It would be absurd to address the issue of marriage and not include sex. Unless a fellow has some type of medical problem or a psychological condition that causes him to be uninterested in sex, it is usually at the forefront of his mind. For that reason, I want to fight through the awkwardness of the subject and be candid about it.

The best advice I can give my son regarding the sexual union between a husband and wife is that he must always remember that to offer her the best experience possible, sex should be a *progressive* event. I like to compare it to shifting gears in a standard transmission vehicle. To start in "high" gear is a serious mistake.

Not long after I acquired my first motorcycle, I took Annie for a ride. Having limited opportunity to learn how to handle a passenger, I was preoccupied with keeping the bike from tipping over. When we came to a stop sign, the grade was slightly uphill. I was so involved in not stalling the motor that I forgot to shift into first before we stopped. When the highway was clear we started to move forward. The engine revved but the fifth gear could not handle the load. The engine strained and died. We started rolling backward, so I squeezed the brake lever. The bike started to tip. At that moment, Annie responded to her natural tendency to put her feet down to keep from falling. When she did, one of her bare legs touched the hot exhaust pipe. The result was a nasty burn as her skin bubbled under the heat.

What does this have to do with sex? When a fellow gets caught up in passion and attempts to go to top gear with his wife, things can easily stall out. While he likely knows what to do when a gasoline engine sputters, sometimes husbands are not so quick to remember that when it comes to sex, wives need them to start in first, or low, gear.

This is where Philippians 2 comes back into play: "Consider your wife's needs as more important than your own" (my paraphrase of verse 3). When a man puts his wife's fulfillment on the top line of his list of priorities, he creates an environment for quality passion. Putting the vehicle in *first gear* can be done by understanding and acting out the wisdom found in the old adage, "Sex begins in the kitchen!"

The implication of this quip is not that he should clear out a place on the linoleum by moving the table and chairs out of the way. Instead, it suggests that he be attentive to her needs outside the bedroom so she will feel loved for who she is, not what she is. Doing the dishes, taking out the trash, gassing up her car, mulching her garden, and cleaning the windows are all considered part of sensual foreplay by a woman. It's hard for some guys to believe this, but if they would just ask their gals, they would discover it is true!

Second gear is reached when the husband approaches sex with sensitivity to his wife's schedule or energy level. Trying to get things rolling after her eyes are drooping with exhaustion is not a good idea. A tired woman is rarely a willing or enthusiastic participant in the physical union.

Shifting into *third gear* is a matter of privacy and safety. If your kids, for example, are nearby, it is normally not in her nature to give complete attention to the experience. It's not that she is a bad lover; instead, it's because she is a good mother. While a man may find excitement at any given moment, conditions need to be right for a woman. A husband who makes it his job to arrange for the most private of intimate times with his wife will find their time together much more enjoyable.

Fourth gear has several teeth in it: 1) consistently going to bed at the same time she does *only* when a husband wants "something" is a turn off for the wife. Being careful to be between the sheets with her just to talk is wise; 2) another tooth in the gear is maintaining good hygiene. Showering, smelling good, brushing teeth, washing hair, and so on are always advised before getting "close" to a woman; 3) understanding what turns her off is as important as knowing what turns her on. Some women fiercely dislike certain sexual activities. She should be asked what these might be and if she reveals such information, the husband should avoid them like a plague. If he doesn't, the engine may be violently thrown into reverse.

Fifth gear. Once all other gears are shifted carefully and in the right order, let nature take its course.

The marriage acrostic we just went through presents a lot of information. In no way, of course, does it fully cover the issue of a man and his marriage. Besides, when it comes to being a husband, it seems that the more I learn, the less I know. I *can* say that my journey with my wife has been my favorite part of life. I will be forever grateful that God didn't leave me alone. I want my son to know that perhaps the grandest sunrise he will ever see will be on the morning of the day he is scheduled to put on a tuxedo, pin a corsage to his lapel, and stand at the front of the church to watch his bride enter the room. With God, his family, and his friends as his witness, he can be glad for the moment when he can finally say, "Then comes marriage…"

7

Then Comes Son
with a Baby Carriage

"For no man can lay a foundation other than the one which is laid, which is Jesus Christ" (1 Corinthians 3:11). I want my son to know that leading him to a relationship with Jesus was the first step in making him a "building" where God would care to dwell. When it comes his turn to build and he has laid the foundation of Christ in his children's hearts, he must be very careful how he builds on it. As a dad, this will be his most sobering responsibility.

If you are a father, you are a builder....

I've had some scary moments in my life. Car wrecks, an airplane engine quitting in midflight, a rattlesnake invading my space, and a painful plunge from high in a tree while deer hunting to name just a few. While some unexpected things have shaken my comfort level, it was an expected event that brought the most anxiety—the arrival of our first newborn.

What was I afraid of? When Nathan was an infant, I was scared I was going to drop him and break his little bones. I was also anxious about getting pooped on—or worse, not catching the "movement" in time to keep it off of Annie's prize quilt she'd told me not to use for a changing blanket. (That, my friend, is *real* fear!) I was also frightened to death by the idea of being responsible for a tiny human being. It wasn't so much the physical care that unnerved me. I learned rather quickly how to do things like swipe the brown stuff off a baby's rear end with premoistened wipes, apply a generous splat of Desonex, pin on a diaper without attaching it to the child's skin, and work a pacifier into a little mouth that was squalling louder than a jet engine. Just about anybody can master those chores.

What scared me most wasn't taking care of the outside of the kid—it was the inside, his soul and spirit. I was keenly aware that God had placed into my care the smallest, most innocent, and most impressionable of His creation. And even more serious, the hour would someday come when He would call the child back to Himself and divinely assess his condition. I knew that if my son reached his adult years, how he used his free will would have the greatest bearing on God's final determination of his soul. I also understood that it was my job as a parent to help Nathan appreciate the weightiness of such a reality. My time to accomplish this eternally important task had its limitations. With that in mind, I was shaking in the fear of God. Having had no previous experience as a dad, I was horrified.

The closer Annie got to her delivery date, the shorter my nails got. As I nibbled on the remaining nubs, Nathan came kicking into the world. I had no choice but to face head-on the job of being his papa. As I watched the nurses clean his little body and prepare to lay him in his mother's arms, a stark reality hit me: There is a major difference between *becoming* a dad and *being* a dad. If the former is caused by being drunk with passion, the latter is the coffee that sobers you up. My son's arrival in March 1977 certainly made me want to walk a straight line.

When we took him home, I tried not to let my nervousness show. In fact, I am confident that the joy I was feeling over the arrival of our little one more than covered the fear I was feeling. No one seemed to notice or mention that I had lost weight and looked a little anemic. As far as I know, I had managed to keep my composure. Yet my heart raced each time I thought of the likelihood that the next 18 to 25 years would require more of me than I could supply. I struggled quietly and deeply until...one day I heard something that made the sun rise once again in my heart.

I will never forget the hope that rushed in when I heard someone say, "If God has been kind enough to make you a 'builder of little temples' where He wants to dwell, He is also compassionate enough to give you the tools to be that builder." I cannot describe the comfort my soul felt when I realized that when I was called to the job as a father/carpenter, I was given a full toolbox. Up until that day, I had never seen myself as a builder; therefore, I didn't even know I had the tools.

As I pondered the revelation that had brought a holy calm into my new role as dad, I began to inventory the tools I could use through the years. The following lyric was written to list a few of them.

Tools for the Trade

If you are a father, you are a builder
And your children will become what you've made
Please do your best, and please don't forget
God gave you the tools for the trade

He gave you *eyes* to see where your child might go wrong
And *feet* to lead them safely through
Hands to hold their hands
And *lips* to say, "I love you"

He gave you *arms* to hold them when they are afraid
Time to wait until they're calm
Ears to hear between their lines
Tears to cry when they're gone

And your *knees* are for playing
And they're also for praying
That God will watch over the child
And in those times you can't say it
But they still need to hear it
You can say "I love you" with your *smile*

If you are a father, you are a builder
And your children will become what you've made
Please don't forget so that you can do your best
God gave you the tools for the trade [11]

Today, the little bundle of joy I once cradled in my arms could easily carry me over his broad shoulders. He has reached that time in his life when, not too far away in the future, he, too, could find himself eating fingernail sandwiches as he faces fatherhood. That being possible, I want him to know that even though there is little I can do to completely stop him from feeling the jitters about becoming a "builder," he can find comfort in the God who provides the tools.

Using the "Tools for the Trade" lyric, I want to offer some helpful guidance to my son should he someday hear himself referred to as "dad." I hope he will not only see just how wise God is in His equipment provision, but also how incredibly practical the tools are. Amazingly, most of them are permanently attached to our bodies. How much more convenient could He make it for us?

Eyes

God has given dads two eyes of flesh with which to see danger before a child does. With this pair we can see in the physical realm what an immature child might miss because he is either unable to comprehend or too distracted to pay attention. When Nathan was a toddler he was with us on a concert tour in a southern, coastal state. The evening meal was enjoyed at the home of a friend's mother. As we visited with her in the kitchen prior to suppertime, I saw my son through the window as he walked around in the fenced-in backyard. Suddenly my eyes caught sight of a familiar mound of dirt that he was approaching and, without hesitating or excusing myself, I darted out the door and ran to my son. From experience, I knew what pain awaited in the loose, sandy heap. It was the nest of a colony of fire ants! Had I paused for a few seconds, or worse, not been watching, the evening could have turned out disastrous for my little one.

In addition to two natural eyes, God also gives a dad the all-important spiritual eyes. As a child gets older and develops his own sense of physical danger, the need for dad's protective peepers grows less. However, the need for his father's alert vision for spiritual danger increases drastically. It is then that

Philippians 1:9 becomes a parental imperative: "And this I pray, that your love may abound still more and more in real knowledge and all discernment." A dad desperately needs these "extra eyes" that can see the unseen.

"Real knowledge" is the kind that enables us to avoid the error of moral misconduct. It is connected to the salvation experience. When a dad has entrusted himself to Christ, the Lord blesses him with a quiet confirmation in his heart, as described in Romans 8:16: "The Spirit Himself bears witness with our spirit that we are children of God" (NKJV). The moment a temptation comes that urges us to disobediently stray, there arises the supernatural reminder, "You are God's child. Don't go there!" Until a youngster understands and embraces this marvelous knowledge that comes from the Holy Spirit of Christ, his dad needs to be ready to see the danger for him and lead him to a righteous choice.

A good picture of this inner alertness in a dad took place in the laundry room of Annie's parents' house. Nathan and I had come in from a hunt and, in his rush to get to the dinner table to enjoy some of his grandmother's cooking, he hurried into the "back room" and leaned his gun against the door facing. He started to dart into the kitchen when something prompted me to ask, "Nathan, did you unload your gun like you're supposed to do before you came inside?" Sure enough, he had failed to empty the five, high-powered 30-30 shells and put them into the safety of his pocket. His lack of compliance to the "empty your rifle rule" may have been a result of a distraction caused by his anxiousness to get to the dinner table, but it was a potentially tragic misuse of a privilege. Both of us shuddered to think of how many little grandkids were running in and out of the house through that same room.

That quiet whisper in my heart to prompt Nathan to check his gun is a vivid illustration of how the voice of the

Spirit of God can softly compel a dad to check out what a son may be doing or not doing. By not ignoring that God-given intuitiveness, Nathan was kept safe that day and alerted to the importance of being more careful. He was so deeply disturbed by his potentially fatal mistake that to this day he triple-checks his weapon when we come in from a hunt or before we get into a truck.

The second eye, "discernment," is a perception based on experience. Going back to Nathan and the pile of dirt, I had, at one time, felt the sting of a small army of fire ants. I knew firsthand what excruciating pain my son was doomed to feel if he stepped in or fell into the mound. The fire ant dance is not fun! But deeper than the skin of flesh, I have also known the hurt in the spirit that results from a willful participation in sin.

When I was a kid, I stole a toy car from our neighborhood hardware store. It wasn't fun to be parentally escorted back to the presence of the store owner to confess my wrongdoing. That experience, along with a host of other paddle prances I endured as a child after "falling short of the glory of God," managed to convince me that one way or the other, payment must be made for sin. Knowing personally the painful consequences of getting tangled up with "disobedieants" (sorry, I couldn't resist), I was more than willing to use the eyes God gave me to help my son avoid his own demise.

Feet

It was not enough just to see the "fire ant" danger Nathan was headed to in our friend's backyard; I also had to be willing to do something about it. I wasn't at all apologetic for suddenly darting out the back door. It didn't matter to me that my good manners fell by the wayside. Much more important to me was getting to my toddler and guiding him away from the infested mound. This can also apply to "spiritual" feet.

If a dad is going to lead a child around the dangerous obstacles of moral failure, he must first know where he is going. In his heart, the father must allow his own steps to be "ordered by the Lord." A father who is submitted to the pursuit of righteousness can confidently say, "Hear, my son, and accept my sayings and the years of your life will be many. I have directed you in the way of wisdom; I have led you in upright paths. When you walk, your steps will not be impeded; and if you run, you will not stumble" (Proverbs 4:10-12). A child whose dad has a heart that contains the law of God should consider himself blessed to have a parent who will guide him to the Father in heaven.

With a heart of deep gratitude, I can say that my Dad has been very careful in the steps he has taken through the years. As a result, I know his footprints are safe to follow. The lyric below commends him for his diligence to righteous living.

Daddy's Shoes

Daddy's shoes made a deep impression
In that West Virginia snow
I put my feet where he was steppin'
He made a real good path to follow
And he led me home that winter day
Back in 1955
That was years ago
But I can say
That in this heart of mine

I'm still steppin' in the tracks
Of my daddy's shoes

It's a trail I love to follow
'Cause it'll lead me through
And when life gets cold and bitter
I'll just do what I saw him do
I'll make it safely home someday
Steppin' in the tracks of my daddy's shoes [12]

"Truly, truly, I say to you, the Son can do nothing of Himself, unless it is something He sees the Father doing…" (John 5:19). This sobering insight into the way Jesus viewed His relationship with His heavenly Father should motivate any God-fearing dad to cautiously choose the path he is walking because his children will more than likely be right behind him.

Hands

Some of the best TV or movie drama is created when someone is dangling over the side of a steep cliff, reaching desperately for the hand of a would-be rescuer. As the fingers of both actors stretch to their limits and the music builds, the viewer anxiously cringes as the two hands inch toward each other. Oh, how sweet is the relief that is felt when the hands connect!

Sooner or later a child will spiritually fall. How do I know? Psalm 37:23 makes it clear that "when [not if] he falls, he will not be hurled headlong, because the LORD is the One who holds his hand." "Hand" refers to strength. When a dad grips the hand of a fallen son, he is essentially passing his own power to his child. In the same way a rescuer lends strength to the one hanging over the side of a cliff, a dad can restore the hopes of moral survival into his son's life by extending the hand of forgiveness and fellowship. What a beautiful picture this is of our loving, heavenly Father, who reaches for the hand of one of His own who has stumbled.

Not only can a dad's hands be instruments of deliverance from danger, his hands can also be the place where a child can know tenderness. Some of my most memorable moments with my kids have been when we were walking along and I felt their little hands slip into mine. To wrap my longer fingers around their tiny palms would send the warmth of acceptance up my emotional spine. Their love for their "papa" and their desire to connect with me was a precious thing. I know my touch also reassured them that they were loved and safe.

I remember one particular moment in my childhood that stays with me even to this day. At 50+ years, I still recall the old 1956 Ford that my dad owned. I was standing on the backseat and leaning over the front just behind him. With my chin nearly on his shoulder, he reached back over me and with a strong hand gently stroked the back of my head. It only lasted a half-minute or so but I still know how it felt. His hand sliding softly across my head was a sentence: "Son, you're welcome to be close to me anytime you want." I want my son to know that hands can say those kind of words.

Lips

The lips are the last in the line of the intricate connections that make up the human's communication device. While lips are the door that words pass through, they are not the place where words are formed. That happens in the heart: "For the mouth speaks out of that which fills the heart" (Matthew 12:34). The lips release the overflow of the inner thoughts of a person. For that reason, when a child hears his dad say "I love you," the youngster is mysteriously and wonderfully *connected* to the heart of his father. What a wonderful tool available to dads!

While there are many words that kids love to hear, such as, "Let's go outside and play" or "Let's open our presents," the three words that will always mean the most are "I love you." Proverbs 10:21 is a great verse for dads to remember: "The lips of the righteous feed many." Like a good, wholesome meal is to the body, so are the kind words of a father to the soul of a child.

To be sure, a man must be careful how he speaks to his son. King David begged in Psalm 141:3, "Set a guard, O LORD, over my mouth; keep watch over the door of my lips." He must have known that just behind that "door" was a potential monster called the tongue. It is not only referred to as a fire that can destroy great forests, it is also called a "sharp sword" and a "deadly arrow" (see James 3; Psalm 57:4; Jeremiah 9:8).

Knowing that harm or harmony can fly out of the "door," how utterly important it is to speak words that honor God and fit the moment. I want my son to know that the most effective use of his lips, and the tongue that lies just behind them, is accomplished when he follows the wisdom of Proverbs 8:6 and 15:23: "Listen, for I will speak noble things; and the opening of my lips will reveal right things"; "a man has joy in an apt answer, and how delightful is a timely [appropriate] word." Anything less will result in the destruction, instead of the construction, of a son's willingness to follow a dad as he leads him to a relationship with Christ.

Arms

There's something strange, but gloriously comforting about a hug from a dad, especially when fear has gripped the heart of a child. Without saying a word, confidence is exchanged. The father seems to absorb his child's anxiety and a calmness comes over the young one. When my kids were younger a thunderstorm would sometimes roll into our area. As the earth rattled and the brilliant strobe of lightning flashed through the house, the kids would run to where I was sitting and jump into my lap. I took great joy in wrapping my arms around them. When I would hold their little heads next to my chest, their pounding hearts would soon stop racing as I displayed an air of confidence that everything was going to be all right.

If the storm was particularly fierce, I would often enlist the use of another tool to help my kids feel safe...

Time

Patiently waiting to feel their little bodies relax was some of the best togetherness moments we have experienced. Crisis times can be very useful to a dad who wants to teach his child that later in life he will find peace in the midst of trouble by spending time in his heavenly Father's arms.

As my children grew older, the storms took on a different form: failed grades, smashed bumpers, missed shots at big white-tail bucks, and, far worse, the loss of grandparents. Though our embraces were only temporary, I always tried to make my arms an available hiding place. I hope my son will know that his arms, too, can be a refuge someday for his children.

Ears

A dad's ability to listen has to go far beyond the ears of flesh. He has to detect what is really said by a child even when his thoughts are not clearly verbalized. Having these kinds of listening devices is similar to one of my favorite tools that

I use when attempting to hang a heavy picture on a drywall surface: a "stud finder." The older type uses a little post magnet that is mounted to the center of a cradle and allowed to swing freely. It is used to find the hidden nails that hold the drywall to a wooden stud. To do so, the tool is slid over the surface of the wall until the small magnet stands to attention. The interaction between the magnet and the metal of the nail reveals the location of the stud.

In a similar way, as we communicate with our kids, we must learn to listen closely and prayerfully in order to understand what lies just under the surface of a child's facial or body expressions. Once we detect the "real issue" behind his wall of flesh, then we've found something solid to which we can attach the truth that is appropriate for the situation. Job 12:11 puts it this way: "Does not the ear test words, as the palate tastes its food?" I want my son to know that this is one talent he will need to develop if he becomes a father. Without it, he will miss some of the deepest feelings buried in the hearts of his children.

Tears

Tears speak, too. When Nathan was born, the droplets of joy fell from our cheeks, silently saying, "Welcome, Son!" Nearly as quickly as it took for those wet beads to fall to the floor, the years passed and the tears of farewell washed across our faces. (It seemed that fast anyway!) Nathan's absence is evidenced by an upstairs room that once shook with the pounding of bass woofers that rhythmically reported his energetic taste in music. His bedroom now stands like a vault that holds only memories. Someday, if the Lord tarries His coming and my son says his hellos and goodbyes to his own children, he'll understand the wordless way tears can talk.

As it turned out, both Nathan and our daughter Heidi went to college about the same time. Nathan, the oldest, delayed his departure due to his post high-school involvement in the recording industry. Consequently, our house emptied rather abruptly and the misty eyes caught both Annie and me off-guard. As a means of therapy, the following lyric was written...

It's Much Too Quiet 'Round Here

Where is the music that rattled the floor
Where is the angry slam of the door
Where are the questions, "Why?" and "What for?"
It's much too quiet 'round here.

Where is the fighting that drove us mad
Where are the conversations we had
Where are the cries of happy and sad
It's much too quiet 'round here

How sweet is the sound of a child in the home
Guess we assumed it would go on and on
We never dreamed it would one day be gone
It's much too quiet 'round here

Where are the footsteps out in the hall
The telephone hardly rings at all
Your absence is noticed inside these walls
It's much too quiet 'round here

Love has a voice
And sometimes when it speaks
It sounds like a child making noise

How sweet is the sound of a child in the home
Guess we assumed it would go on and on

We never dreamed you would one day be gone
Now it's much too quiet 'round here.[13]

Knees

When I was in my mid-thirties and training for a marathon I planned to complete in my fortieth year, Annie kept warning me, "Those knees were meant to last a lifetime. You'd better treat them kindly!" Of course, she was right. Three months after my marathon dream came true, the nightmare of knee surgery woke me to reality. Today, my running has been reduced to a pitiful hobble.

Often when my knees ache they talk to me. First of all, they remind me of how sweet my wife is to rarely offer a rightly deserved, "I told you so." Second, I fondly recall the painless participation my young joints experienced as I played with my kids on the ground, on the carpet, and even on concrete.

Those unforgettable days gave way to the delight of eye-level recreation. Hiking, climbing, basketball games, and hide-and-seek are a few of the other activities my pathetic old knees recall. Their creaking even testifies to the 500-mile and 250-mile bike rides I took with Nathan and Heidi.

Of all that my noisy knees say, perhaps the most important is the reminder to pray for my children. If I am never able to pedal another mile, climb another mountain on the Appalachian Trail, or run the bases in our little backyard Wiffle ball field, I know I can always use my knees in this far more significant way. As Colossians 4:2 says, "Devote yourselves to prayer, keeping alert in it with an attitude of thanksgiving." And if I ever wear my knees totally out, thankfully, I will always have the knees of my heart.

Smile

A smile is a hug without arms. It's a love note that can be sent airmail to the stage where a kid is nervously performing or out on a basketball court where a son has made only one of two free throws. A smile is a hand that can reach all the way to right field and congratulate a kid for a one-hop throw that almost made it to the second baseman. A smile can even jump off of a picture and give a lipless kiss of love to a soldier 2000 miles away. A father's smile is the light that glows in the window of his face that says, "You're always welcome in my heart." Sometimes that's all a child needs!

A Bonus Tool

There's one more tool that is available to help dads construct little houses of God: God's great outdoors.

From the backyard with little children (be careful for those heaps of loose, sandy dirt!) to the remote mountains of faraway places with young adults, God's creation is an incredible way to inform kids about their Maker. Romans 1:20 says it best: "For since the creation of the world His invisible attributes, His eternal power and divine nature, have been clearly seen, being understood through what has been made, so that they are without excuse."

I want my son to remember that as a dad, he can spend as little as an hour and zero money, to weeks and a month's salary on outdoor adventures with his kids. (For outdoor activities and suggestions, see my *A Look at Life from God's Great Outdoors* [Harvest House].) Whatever investment is made, I can guarantee that not a minute or day, a dime or a dollar will be wasted. Why? Because the return is priceless— especially when your child wants to come and spend time with you, even when you're too old to go outside and play.

8

The Guard

"Now concerning everything which I have said to you, be on your guard; and do not mention the name of other gods, nor let them be heard from your mouth." This command, given in Exodus 23:13, serves to further enforce what God said to His people in an earlier, more familiar passage:

> You shall have no other gods before Me. You shall not make for yourself an idol, or any likeness of what is in heaven above or on the earth beneath or in the water under the earth. You shall not worship them or serve them; for I, the LORD your God, am a jealous God, visiting the iniquity of the fathers on the children, on the third and the fourth generations of those who hate Me, but showing lovingkindness to thousands, to those who love Me and keep My commandments. You shall not take the name of the LORD your God in vain, for the LORD will not leave him unpunished who takes His name in vain (Exodus 20:3-7).

I want my son to know that God's divine jealousy for those who wear His matchless name extends even to him. Because of this incredible blessing, Nathan must remain on-guard against the enemies that would profane the excellency of our Savior's holy name.

I'll never forget my first experience at being a guard. It was a late afternoon in January of 1970. I was one among a busload of Navy recruits who were dumped onto the parking lot of the Great Lakes Naval Basic Training Center near Chicago. There to greet us was a uniformed gentleman who wore a menacing smile. As we vigorously shuffled our freezing feet and blew warm breath into our ungloved hands, we were suddenly shocked by the foghorn-level sound of our host's rough and unfriendly voice: "Line up in columns of two, you monkeys!"

To this day, I distinctly remember the sinking feeling that rushed through me when our appointed leader barked his orders that were so bitterly seasoned with unkindness. In that instant I realized that my spirit, which had been fancy-free just the moment before, was now crushed and captured by the mighty hand of the military. Somehow the recruiter's friendly appeal only two months earlier failed miserably in revealing the harsh reality of what awaited my life at the end of the bus ride. I instantly knew I had made a really bad mistake...and I didn't appreciate being called a monkey!

I was not alone in my bewildered reaction to the officer who had rattled our civilian cages. Fear gripped all of us as we silently asked ourselves, "What is a column of two?" For a few seconds we looked at each other for the answer. Then we looked at the man who knew very well we didn't have a clue about what to do. As if he assumed that a higher volume would result in a deeper understanding of his words, he repeated himself. The painful tone of his obvious disgust with us was really disheartening. Everyone wanted to please the man, but we didn't know how.

I'm not sure if grabbing and throwing new recruits is prohibited in the pages that contain the code of military conduct, but if it was, our leader had not read that book. Within
20 seconds he had 30 or more "Gomer Pyles" standing in
formation like a group of "Sergeant Carters." To be honest,
I was impressed with us. He wasn't, of course. As he
instructed us to follow him into the gates that led us to the
demise of our independence, he said something about left
and right. When he did, some of us went left and some went
right, just as he had ordered. That really set him off.

The next hour was beyond interesting. It was frightening.
With each passing minute I plunged deeper and deeper into
regret, fear, and homesickness. The evening ended without
my standard, late-night tradition of a bowl of cereal and some
TV time with Johnny Carson. I felt completely deserted even
though I was in a barracks filled with a fresh crop of ship-
mates.

As I was preparing for some needed rest in my narrow,
unfamiliar bed, I suddenly got a firm tap on the shoulder. I
turned around to find a uniformed stranger vigorously
curling his index finger at me. He said, "You, sailor, come
with me."

What had I done wrong? I wondered quietly. Having had
no previous experience with what goes on behind the walls of
a military base, I nervously followed the fellow. I assumed I
was about to be sacrificed to some god of the spirits of
drowned sailors. Much to my relief, what he wanted was for
me to take the first watch at the front door. All I had to do,
he said, was stand there at parade rest (parade what?) and be
prepared to alert all the other sailors if an officer was entering
the building.

I had only one worry when he left me standing there
alone. I didn't really know what an officer looked like and, as

far as I was concerned, everyone on the base except those of us who had just arrived was a high-ranking sailor. The only thing I knew to do was to not take any chances. If the door opened and someone entered, I was going to consider them salute-worthy.

Thirty minutes passed on my one hour of guard duty. I was grateful for no activity, and by then, everyone was quiet and had settled in for a night's sleep. The lights were out except for the red glow of the exit sign above me. Suddenly, I heard the sound of footsteps on the wooden stairs that led into our barracks. My heart raced with excited fear that I was about to be tested in my skills as a watchman. Desperately not wanting to do the wrong thing and be scolded by the "brass," I squinted my eyes in an effort to see who was opening the door. Because of the light conditions the person was merely a silhouette.

Without hesitating, I let out a crowd-rousing, blood-curdling command: "Attention on Deck!" (Those were the words I was told to say if an officer came for a visit.) In one ear I heard the thunderous sound of nearly 200 bare feet hitting the barracks floor. It was accompanied by the noise of grunts, groans, and low screams as the wakened recruits stepped on one another's toes while scrambling in the dark to find their way to the foot of their bunks.

In the other ear I heard the following words from the person who had entered the building: "Hey! You idiot! (Actually, "idiot" is not the name he used.) I've only been here two days. I'm one of you. They've got me doing security rounds." When I realized I had jumped the gun and failed to identify the visitor as a mere underling, my whole body turned red with embarrassment. I hated to step into the bunk area and announce the news that it was a false alarm, but I knew if I didn't all the guys who were just as nervous as I was would stand there at attention until dawn.

Reluctantly, I stuck my head into the large, unlit room and said with a left-handed wave and an apologetic tone, "Sorry, fellows. False alarm. You can go back to bed!"

As they mumbled and climbed back under their covers, I took my post once again. While the next half hour crept by I thought back over the day. I realized that in one short evening my social status had been reduced to the classification of a stupid monkey and, among other things, I had been accused of having a dog for a mother.

Time went on and I graduated from boot camp, spent two years on an aircraft carrier, and was discharged nearly three years later. All in all, it wasn't too bad a deal. I finally learned how to fold my briefs and T-shirts, how to quickly wash a shipload of dishes, and even how to clean a head (bathroom) so spotless that you could eat off the floor (notice I said "you"!). As it turned out, I can honestly say I am one stupid monkey who was glad for the experience.

I Joined the Army!

Only four years later, after completing nearly three years of the U.S. Navy, I joined the army. It was not the armed forces of Uncle Sam; I enlisted in the army of God. On that unforgettable morning in March 1974, I willingly allowed Him to strip my heart of its sin-stained garments and accepted the uniform of the righteousness of Christ. It was the smartest move I have ever made.

It's as if the Holy Spirit tapped me on the shoulder and said, "Young soldier, come with me." I respectfully followed, and He led me to the entrance of my heart. There He instructed me with the words found in 1 Peter 5:6-8:

Humble yourselves under the mighty hand of God, that He may exalt you at the proper time, casting all your anxiety upon Him, because He cares for you. Be of sober spirit, be on the alert. Your adversary, the devil, prowls around like a roaring lion, seeking someone to devour. But resist him, firm in your faith.

One of my first and main duties as a soldier of the cross was, amazingly enough, being a watchman. Not unlike the guard duty I was appointed to that first night at Great Lakes, the responsibility I now have must be taken very seriously. I am not free to grow faint, and nothing should be allowed to enter unless clearly identified as holy. I didn't fully know the depth of the responsibility in the hour I was ordered to begin my spiritual duty. Yet I accepted the post. And even though I have given in to drowsiness at times, I have endeavored to be faithful.

Many other soldiers have joined God's army of believers since I enlisted long ago. One of them happens to be my own son. He is a fine young comrade. He has, like all who enlist in this great band of troops, received his orders to stand guard. Having been in "uniform" a few years longer than he, I want to use my veteran experience to inform him of two areas of our relationship with the Lord our Commander that especially need to be watched over. If these sectors are kept free from an invasion of the adversary, the strength of the entire fort can be maintained.

Guard the Name of God

First of all, I want my son to know that it is imperative that he stand firm at the gate of his heart as a protector of the matchless name of Christ. One of the reasons why this must become an utmost priority is found in the apostle Peter's declaration recorded in Acts 4:12: "And there is salvation in no one else; for there is no other name under heaven that has been given among men by which we must be saved." Because our salvation from eternal destruction is found *only in Christ*, His name should be held in the highest esteem. To those of us who place our complete trust in the finished work He accomplished through the pain of His crucifixion, the despair of His burial, and His glorious resurrection, His name is far too precious to allow it to be defamed.

I want my son to consider the weight of these words written about our Savior in Paul's letter to the Colossians:

> For in [Christ] all the fullness of Deity dwells in bodily form, and in Him you have been made complete, and He is the head over all rule and authority; and in Him you were also circumcised with a circumcision made without hands, in the removal of the body of the flesh by the circumcision of Christ; having been buried with Him in baptism, in which you were also raised up with Him through faith in the working of God, who raised Him from the dead. And when you were dead in your transgressions and the uncircumcision of your flesh, He made you alive together with Him, having forgiven us all our transgressions, having canceled out the certificate of debt consisting of decrees against us, which was hostile to us; and He has taken it out of the way, having nailed it to the cross (2:9-14).

And in his letter to the Galatians Paul declares, "I have been crucified with Christ; and it is no longer I who live, but Christ lives in me; and the life which I now live in the flesh I live by faith in the Son of God, who loved me and gave Himself up for me" (2:20).

What a glorious day it is when the life-saving truth of our redemption through Christ finally makes it through our minds and settles in our spirits! And when we finally understand that we can love Him "because He first loved us," it is no wonder that we are unwilling to tolerate anyone or anything that would try to profane Him. While the rest of the world may refuse to take Him seriously, we stand ready to proclaim with the psalmist David, "O LORD, our Lord, how majestic is Your name in all the earth" (Psalm 8:1).

In order to help Nathan remember the incredible value of God's name, I taught him to "practice" the absence of blasphemy. For example, the "rule of tongue" in our home was to avoid using slang words that even resembled the name of God, such as "gosh," "golly," or "gee whiz." I know these terms don't stoop to the depths of profanity that others may reach. However, each time the mental effort was made to avoid them, the discipline triggered a reminder in his heart that God's name is too important to even remotely disrespect it. I realized Nathan was getting this message the day he returned the favor and called me on the "wrong word" carpet. I was thrilled when he did it. Not only was he getting the idea, I also realized I had a "brother in Christ" who would help me when I verbally stumbled.

Another tactic I introduced to our family when Nathan was very young was carefully screening any movies we would see. We didn't have internet sites, such as www.screenit.com, to help us know in advance exactly what language the film contained, but we researched, and if we learned that God's name was taken in vain in the movie, it was eliminated as a candidate for entertainment.

Admittedly, it was not an easy standard to keep. The peer pressure the kids endured was difficult and, to be honest, I wanted to see some of the movies we missed. Our alternative was to wait and, eventually, the TV version would be released. (For the most part, these were "cleaned up" sufficiently.) In the end, we were better off for having waited. The bottom line is that the name of Christ who loves us supremely and who will remain long after films have burned to ashes is far too precious to knowingly endorse its blatant misuse.

I want Nathan to know that even with this kind of "practice," there will be times when he might be guilty of spiritually "nodding off" during his watch. Thankfully, God's love for us does not waver. This was illustrated in my life by an unforgettable reminder that in God's army, I am not my own, because I was "bought with a price."

A business opportunity presented itself that had the potential to generate some significant additional income for our family. To participate, I had to step outside the boundary of the specific work God had called me to and walk into an area that I knew was not completely sanctified. Still, I made what I thought was a safe offer.

A few days later I was scheduled to have a phone meeting with the powers-that-be at the company to find out if I was "in." As it turned out, when the hour came to make the call I was bush-hogging on a tractor for a friend. I shut the motor off and dialed the number on my cell phone. Under the shade of a tree at the edge of a huge meadow, I heard, "Sorry, Mr. Chapman, your offer was not accepted."

I was crushed. As I sat and stared across the field and nursed my wounded ego, I evaluated the outcome. I questioned the quality of my offer as well as myself: *How could they have refused me?* I wondered. I felt utterly rejected. Suddenly, as though a still, small voice hovered over my shoulder and softly spoke into my ear, the following words poured into my heart. I quickly dug for a pen and notepad and wrote them down.

You Belong to Me

I almost gave my devotion away
To someone who lives in the dark
But Jealous Divine
He found me in time
And whispered in my heart

"You belong to me, you belong to me
Not in part but the whole
Body, spirit, and soul
That's the way My love has to be
You belong to Me"

How could I ever forget
For even one moment
What a price for my life that You paid
In the purest way flattered
That my life would matter
I'll cherish the words I heard You say,

"You belong to Me, you belong to Me
Not in part but the whole
Body, spirit, and soul
That's the way My love has to be
You belong to Me"[14]

There, in the privacy of the great outdoors, I read aloud
the words I had just written down. Deep inside I knew God
had spoken. I was overwhelmed when I realized that His
divine jealousy for me was strong enough to reach into time
and space and touch my heart with such a sweet reminder
that He doesn't care to share me with anyone else. The tearful
joy that consumed me in that moment was life-changing.
This is the relentless love I want my son to experience and
understand.

Guard Your Name

I want my son to also know that "a good name is to be more desired than great wealth" (Proverbs 22:1). My take on this passage is that one ounce of personal integrity far outweighs a ton of money. Many criminals have certainly not figured out the power of this truth. They can't seem to understand that it is really tough to maintain credibility when the word "thief" or "lawbreaker" is used in reference to their occupational history. Consequently, they are bitter and rebellious when "real" jobs are hard to come by, credit applications are rejected, and neighbors have a tendency to avoid them. It's important to protect your identity and your name.

"Remember whose child you are!"

I long for Nathan to understand that the very mention of his name will conjure up images of his character in the minds of those who hear it. And just as important to consider is the fact that what others think when they say or hear his name will undeniably influence what they think of his family...and what they think of his God.

My dad was very aware of the fact that my name was more than just a handle he used to pull me to the dinner table. It was a mirror that had the potential to reflect either a good or bad light on me, on him, and on the Savior he so deeply loved. It was for that reason he came up with a statement he repeated over and over to me through the years I lived at home. No matter where I would go, whether to school or just outside to play, he would rarely fail to say, "Remember whose child you are!"

I am now certain that Dad had a twofold purpose for diligently pounding those words into my brain until they reached my heart. One, he was a preacher in a relatively small community in West Virginia where nearly everyone knew everyone else. Believing that a minister's reputation often rides on the back of his children's behavior, Dad was steadfast in his parenting and values. Today, I unreservedly commend him for tending to his own name by faithfully guiding his kids in such a way.

While his own credibility may have been a legitimate concern, I am sure there was a greater purpose in rarely letting me exit the house without hearing his heart's cry. I believe he fearfully embraced the truth found in 2 Corinthians 5:20,21: "Therefore, we are ambassadors for Christ, as though God were making an appeal through us; we beg you on behalf of Christ, be reconciled to God. He made Him who knew no sin to be sin on our behalf, so that we might become the righteousness of God in Him." In addition, Dad understood Psalm 23:3: "He guides me in the paths of righteousness *for His name's sake*" (emphasis added).

My father believed that if God was so seriously concerned about His own name, we should, in turn, be considerate enough to guard ours. We should do so with the final goal of bringing glory to the name of God.

During my 19 years in his home, it would be hard to number the times Dad stamped my heart with his plea for me to remember to whom I belonged. I grew to dread hearing his "line" because the convicting truth wore at my sin-prone teen years. But he didn't give up.

By 1970, I had flown out of the nest and landed on the deck of the aircraft carrier *USS Forrestal*. I was surrounded by opportunities to test the "waters of the world." About a year into my military service I found myself standing waist deep, so to speak, in immorality. I was experiencing the "passing pleasures of sin" (Hebrews 11:25). Suddenly, the echo of Dad's words found their way back to my heart. It was not until that moment that I fully realized the depth of my father's plea. At last it took root in my soul. It was that day that I wrote the following lyric.

Remember Whose Child You Are

I'm the son of a mountain preacher
And I'll never say some of the things I've been called
But I knew if I ever did wrong
I'd be the reason my daddy's name would fall

Well, the war, it was raging
And I knew my time to go wasn't very far
And when I left my home up in the mountains
I could hear my daddy say, "Remember whose child
   you are!"

Oh, remember, if you're one of the children
You have a name, wherever you are
Oh, remember, please remember
Remember whose child you are

Well, now I know I've been born again
And my new Father is the one who made the stars
And I know I don't wanna do wrong
'Cause I keep hearing, "Boy, remember whose child
   you are!"

Oh, remember, if you're one of the children
You have a name wherever you are
Oh, remember, please remember
Remember whose child you are![15]

Needless to say, the lasting imprint that Dad's words made on my heart has profoundly affected the way I guard God's name and mine. I have made some very hard choices through the years in order to preserve that integrity. One of the most heart-wrenching decisions came to pass a few years ago. It involved a former employee who was loved by our entire family, especially by Nathan. That element of the situation made it even harder.

The trouble started when it was discovered that the employee was using our company's phone to connect to a "900" number for conversations of a sexual nature. This posed a serious threat to our reputation as well as a potential reproach on the name of Christ. Although it was an excruciating decision, I had to let him go.

As I walked through that valley, Nathan was watching. My highest hopes in the outcome was that he would see that our good name could be put in jeopardy by the behavior of others. When that happens, a good watchman will spring into action and remedy the situation as quickly as possible.

I also want my son to know that time will test the quality of a name that has been well guarded. Proverbs 10:7 reveals, "The memory of the righteous is blessed, but the name of the wicked will rot." Oh, how I desire for the blessing of God's grace to help me live in such a way that when my name is formed on the tongues of those who have known me my memory will be a sweet taste. If this is true, then the greater blessing will be to know that I have not defamed the name of God who has so loved me. This, too, is what I want for my son. May it be so for both of us.

9

Bogeys and Birdies

But the goal of our instruction is love from a pure heart and a good conscience and a sincere faith.

1 TIMOTHY 1:5

A wise and understanding son once said, I used to try to see God through my dad but because of his immoral lifestyle, the image was terribly distorted. However, a drastic change of perspective took place when I yielded my life to Christ. Through my new relationship with Him, I began to see my dad from God's point of view. Today, instead of looking to heaven and being angrily disappointed, I can now look earthward with a compassion and forgiveness.

I want my son to know that all I did for him as a father was motivated by my deep love for him. While I may have done some things right, there are areas where I know I faltered and failed. I am concerned that once he sees these places, the revelation might cause him to question my love for him. May this never be.

On rare occasions I get to enjoy a round of golf. It's always fun to play, but it is doubly delightful when I am with a buddy or two. The best part of my game is on the fairways. Why? Because as the rest of the fellows stand on the greens and wait for me to hack my way to the putting surface, they are feeling really good about themselves. My most valuable contribution to the day is building up the egos of those in my group. I consider it a "ministry."

There is a particular comment I sometimes hear when I am playing golf. It comes from the kind hearts of those who watch my shots drift off the course and into a section that is barely playable. As the ball bounces into the high grass, someone will usually say with a tone of sympathy, "That'll play!"

One day in early June, as I left the tee box and parted ways with my comrades (they went straight down the fairway and I headed to the rough), I heard them utter those words again. As I strolled alone toward my bashful ball, it occurred to me that the often-used remark was more than a compliment—it was mercy. On the 1-to-10 scale of courtesy, it measured a strong 11. In reality, it was a very understanding, "Nice try, Steve. We still like you. Feel free to rejoin us when you can." I am aware that my game reeks, but how grateful I can be when others are kind enough not to point it out.

Later that same month, Father's Day arrived. With it came a very thoughtful greeting card from my son. As I read the rhymed verses that graciously complimented me on the job I had done as a dad, it suddenly occurred to me that my reaction to the sentiments in the card was a little like the feelings I had when my buddies were being kind to me on the golf course. While I am very much aware that I have not done everything correctly, it sure was sweet of Nathan to make me think I did. Though I honestly didn't feel worthy of his praise, the truth is that when it comes to my fatherhood, I'll take a "that'll play" any day over a "can't you do any better than that?"

I am confident that my son's carefully chosen card contained genuine feelings of affection. In no way do I doubt his sincerity. In fact, it is the unselfish goodness he showed me that motivates me to offer him the following apologies. In the same way that the kindness of God leads us to repentance, Nathan's willingness to be forgiving enough to focus on my "good shots" by overlooking my bad ones enables me to recognize and accept the areas of fathering where I feel I have missed the fairway. Even though he doesn't ask for an accounting, I feel the urgency to reveal them so he might better understand any deficits my failures may cause in his life. If he someday becomes a dad and is blessed, as I am, with enough years to see the "back side of the course," he may also feel the need to admit an errant shot or two. Perhaps my willingness to recognize my own slices and hooks will encourage him to do the same.

Following the list of "bogeys" that haunts me as a dad, I will offer a few of the "birdies" I managed to collect in my role as a father. After all, any average golfer knows that if you play long enough, you'll put a ball or two near the hole and get to tap in for that glorious, below-par feeling.

I share these to help others avoid my mistakes and understand that imperfect as we are, as dads we have much to offer our sons.

The Bogeys

Before I show my scorecard with the less than spectacular marks on it, realize that some of these admissions are applicable primarily to my relationship with my son. Even though we may not share the same failures, we are all redeemed through Jesus: "And we know that God causes all things to work together for good to those who love God, to those who are called according to His purpose" (Romans 8:28).

The Word

I want my son to know that I embrace the belief that the Word of God—the Holy Bible, the Old and New Testaments—is our heavenly Father's letter of love and instruction to humankind. As strongly as I believe this, I don't feel I did a good enough job in helping Nathan saturate his heart with its writings.

I was a typical, on-the-go, often preoccupied dad. Yet in the back of my mind there was always the divinely compelling thought, *Don't forget to help your children hide My Word in their hearts.* Whenever I began to feel guilty for my inconsistent attention to this detail, I ran for comfort to God's instructions found in Deuteronomy 6:6-9:

> These words, which I am commanding you today, shall be on your heart. You shall teach them diligently to your sons and shall talk of them when you sit in your house and when you walk by the way and when you lie down and when you rise up. You shall bind them as a sign on your hand and they shall be as frontals on your forehead. You shall write them on the doorposts of your house and on your gates.

The practicality of these instructions was provided for busy dads like me. And because I was not a highly trained, college-degree-holding Bible scholar, I felt a certain freedom to focus on the "teach them on the way" aspect of the passage. As I journeyed with my kids through their growing-up years, I am confident that a respectable amount of truth was learned by observation. However, I can see now that focusing on the "learning while in motion" element of the verses was a little like spraying my sweaty and thirsty kids with the garden hose after they had vigorously played outside on a hot summer day. While they found refreshment in the shower of water, their thirst could be satisfied only by drinking. Although I was careful to pour the principles of God's Word on them by being a living example, I wish I had been more diligent in helping them drink in the Scripture.

It is possible to depend too much on the old adage that "more is caught than taught."

I wish I had encouraged more memorization of Scripture. I wanted Nathan's mind and heart to be so filled with truth that his first reaction to any situation would be filtered through the wisdom of God's Word.

Another activity I could have presented more heartedly was the need for meditating on the Word. Psalm 119:97-104 makes very clear the incredible benefits of "rehearsing" the statutes of God:

> O how I love Your law! It is my meditation all the day. Your commandments make me wiser than my enemies, for they are ever mine. I have more insight than all my teachers, for Your testimonies are my meditation. I understand more than the aged, because I have observed Your precepts. I have

restrained my feet from every evil way, that I may keep Your word. I have not turned aside from Your ordinances, for You Yourself have taught me. How sweet are Your words to my taste! Yes, sweeter than honey to my mouth! From Your precepts I get understanding; therefore I hate every false way.

In the way that a person clears everything off a table to do something that requires space, I regret that I did not help my son remove some of the "fluff" from his schedule so that he could take time to read a passage of Scripture and sit and muse over it. This discipline is not a popular one—in fact, it is almost a lost art in the Christian world. Too many other "stimulants," such as entertainment, technology, and recreation grab at the interests of our kids, and I allowed it to happen. I want my son to know that it is never too late to begin a regular diet of meditation. Even in the face of our overly busy lifestyles, there are creative ways to find that "quiet time" with the Lord.

Many industrious followers of Christ, for example, transform their cars into sanctuaries where they ponder biblical truths during a commute to their jobs. By turning off the radio or ejecting a music CD and replacing it with a CD version of the Bible, some quality time in His Word can be gained. And in some cities the amount of time that can be spent alone with God may be as long as an hour or more! I want my son to know that God will honor anyone who chooses to subtract a few unnecessary obligations in order to add some time for meditation on His Word.

My failure in fostering a regular regimen of in-depth study, memorization, and meditation on the Scriptures was indeed a "ball in the rough." While I am confident that Nathan gained a certain number of important biblical insights by simply observing my walk with Christ, I have learned that it is possible for a dad to depend too much on the old adage that "more is caught than taught." I want my son to know I sincerely apologize for an overdependence on this proverb. As long as he has breath, I hope he strives to continually and actively absorb the Word of God.

Church

Closely connected to having a "life in the Book" is gathering regularly with others who are on the same page. One of the hazards of being musicians is that our travel schedule prohibited us from being consistent attendees of a local congregation. We were usually involved in services somewhere in the nation as guest musicians, but not often enough in our home church to be "sponges" who soaked in the spiritual nourishment of preaching, singing, and regular fellowship. While we go as often as we are in town, occupying our places when the doors were opened—especially on Sundays—was not the norm.

We had a fierce conviction that it would not be good for our children to be left behind when we traveled. Consequently, their seats in the pew were often empty as well. For that reason my children missed the close connections that can develop with church-going peers. Knowing that lifetime friendships result from the ties that bind the saints together, I deeply regret the absence that our vocation inflicted on my children. I hope they sensed our longing to be regulars at a home church.

Even though our infrequent attendance was not intentional, I want my son to know that if his vocation does not require travel, I hope the randomness of his past church experience will not result in his oversight of the admonition found in Hebrews 10:24,25: "And let us consider how to stimulate one another to love and good deeds, not forsaking our own assembling together, as is the habit of some, but encouraging one another; and all the more as you see the day drawing near."

Money

While I am sure I managed to get some good messages across to my son about money—such as the dangers of debt and greed and that contentment is a product of gratitude for what we have, there is one specific missed hit I must confess. By being so generous to him, I may have given him the wrong impression about what he will face in the world that awaits him beyond the walls of the home where he was raised.

I took great delight in giving to my son. One of the reasons I was so quick to keep pouring money into his pockets was because no young man has been more grateful than Nathan. Nearly every time we left a restaurant when we were "on the road," he (as well as his sister, Heidi) would offer a word of thanks to Annie and me for their meals. Each time they did, my heart would be flooded with the warmth of their words.

My son proved over and over that he had learned the lesson about the attitude of gratitude, and I proudly commend him for it. The concern I have, however, is not that he lacks a thankful heart. It is that by lavishing so much upon him I may have given him the impression that the rest of humanity will *want* to do the same.

Anyone who has ventured out of the comfort of their parents' nest and suddenly faced the dog-eat-dog world of the workplace will readily agree that to be prepared for such a shock would be a good thing. For that reason, whenever I gave in abundance to my son, I established an ongoing saying that Nathan learned to expect when he received. As the monetary offerings were handed over, I would say, "This is not the real world!"

My purpose for rubbing this statement into his mind was to make sure he understood that the day would come when my open hands would have to be replaced by his working hands. He needed to know that when it happened, the sum will likely be reduced and his economic life will not be as easy.

Had I not offered the truth that my generosity was not common outside of our house, he might have been among those unfortunate young people who view their work opportunities with much too high an expectation. A good example of this misguided attitude was found in sunny Florida. In one of that state's wealthy communities, the local teens turned up their noses to some jobs that were offered at a soon-to-be-opened fast-food restaurant. Why? Because the allowance that was given by the parents of many of the teenagers exceeded the weekly wage the restaurant was offering. Because they could not find one taker, the owners of the restaurant had to bus their employees in from towns as far away as 50 miles. When I learned of this troubling commentary on those "wealthy" young people, I shivered in fear that I had been a poor parent. Because of that report I questioned whether or not my son had gained a realistic view of money.

One of the best pieces of advice I have ever gleaned about successfully dealing with children and finances came from a radio talk-show host. She received a call from a mother who was seeking wisdom about whether or not to give her newly married son a huge amount of money for the purchase of a major item. The caller was obviously taken aback when the host responded, "Absolutely not!"

It seemed that the generous mother had an underlying fear about seeing her son and new daughter-in-law struggle financially. Though the mom's voice revealed that she was offended that the radio counselor would not see her gift as appropriate, the host strongly urged the worried (and potentially intrusive) mother to let the young people "yearn and earn."

When I heard that clever combination of words, I knew I had come upon a phrase that I would repeat (especially to myself) for the rest of my life. I, too, am sorely tempted to help my now-grown children to never know *want*. However, in my own experience I have found that it is in the yearning that the need for earning is best understood. It is in the midst of yearning that we realize we can get along with less. Knowing how to "make do" until better economic times come along can only be learned through yearning.

As I pondered the talk-show host's words, I thought of the passage found in Matthew 6:8: "For your Father knows what you need before you ask Him." Throughout my son's growing-up years I had been under the errant assumption that if I were going to be a good picture of the heavenly Father to him, one of the things I needed to do was anticipate his needs and make sure they were met *before* he asked. It dawned on me, however, that the passage does not say, "Your Father will *give to you* before you ask." Much to the contrary, the verse clearly indicates that going to the Father and asking is very much a part of the deal. In fact, our needs and longings probably do more to create interaction between us and the Father than anything else in our lives. God is surely pleased when we come to Him with our requests. While He knows of our needs all along, He wants us to show Him that we understand that He is our source for those needs. Our asking is a way of saying, "We need You, Lord!"

In regard to his relationship with his heavenly Father, I want Nathan to not be hesitant to be like the boy I stood beside at a burger joint. He had ordered a cheeseburger, fries, and a large drink. While the young lady behind the counter gathered his food onto a tray, he dug through his pockets for the money to buy it. As he stood there next to me clutching his cash rather tightly, I couldn't help but ask a question. Assuming he might have mowed a few yards or sold a few pop-bottles to collect his currency, I asked, "Is that some hard-earned money you're about to spend?"

I'll never forget how he sort of cleared his throat, shuffled his feet, and bashfully replied, "No, sir, this is some hard-begged money!" My heart melted at the thought of the humility that must have been represented by the bills in his young hand. I want my son to know that even though my days of "it's yours before you ask" are over, my door is always open…and there's nothing wrong with coming to me and asking.

In addition to the "precious pesos" that God supplies when we prayerfully approach Him with a need, I want Nathan to know that some of the most valuable money that will ever pass through his hands is the cash that grows out of diligent and honest labor. In regard to a man's livelihood, Ecclesiastes 2:24 supports the God-honoring act of earning a wage. "There is nothing better for a man than to eat and drink and tell himself that his labor is good. This also I have seen that it is from the hand of God." On the other hand, the Scriptures aren't so kind to the man who refuses to work. First Timothy 5:8 is not a passage I would want to hear in reference to me or to my son: "But if anyone does not provide for his own, and especially for those of his household, he has denied the faith and is worse than an unbeliever."

In light of this sad pronouncement about the slothful, I want my son to know that perhaps the most grievous violation of the noble charge of being a provider is found in those who fall (or jump) into the trap of the "get rich quick" temptation.

In an attempt to bypass the "sweat of the brow," too many people have allowed themselves to become victims of the vultures who prey on the gullible. In 1 Timothy 6:7-10, the apostle Paul warns young Timothy about how a person's insatiable desire for wealth can get him in such trouble:

> For we have brought nothing into the world, so we cannot take anything out of it either. If we have food and covering, with these we shall be content. But those who want to get rich fall [continuously] into temptation and a snare and many foolish and harmful desires which plunge [drag the bottom] men into ruin [corruption] and destruction [unsaved state after death]. For the love of money is a root of all sorts of evil, and some by longing for it have wandered away from the faith and pierced themselves with many griefs.

Tennessee has been successful so far in rejecting a lottery. Though I am not sure if this will remain true, I sincerely hope it will. Some of the saddest sights I have seen have been just across the border in Kentucky. As I wait to pay for gasoline at a convenience mart, I sometimes watch patrons who appear to be almost destitute slap down their hard-earned dollars on the counter in payment for lottery tickets. I cringe as I think of what they are sacrificing for a ridiculously remote chance to skirt the responsibility of working. Their quest for instant wealth is pitiful. How often I have wanted to blurt out, "A fool and his money are easily parted!" Perhaps that's not my role with total strangers. It is, however, my job to guide my son.

Ecclesiastes 5:10 soberly asserts, "He who loves money will not be satisfied with money, nor he who loves abundance with its income. This too is vanity." Understanding the futility of the pursuit of monetary gain leads to embracing the wisdom of 1 Timothy 6:11: "Flee from these things, you man of God, and pursue righteousness, godliness, faith, love, perseverance and gentleness." This list of eternally valuable gains is what I want my son to pursue.

I long for Nathan to know that while he will bring glory to God by making a wage as a provider, true wealth has nothing to do with what jingles in his pockets or the green paper that makes his wallet bulge. As far as money goes, I want him to see and believe the contentment-producing truth in Proverbs 30:8,9: "Keep deception and lies far from me, give me neither poverty nor riches; feed me with the food that is my portion, that I not be full and deny You and say, 'Who is the LORD?' Or that I not be in want and steal, and profane the name of my God."

Household and Vehicle Maintenance

When Annie and I married in 1975, we had nothing. (And after all these years we have managed to keep most of it!) One of the things we didn't possess was a house full of appliances. (That's the bad news. The good news is I didn't have to fix them!) Time went on and the accumulation process started. Suddenly I was living among items that had motors, belts, switches, filters, nuts and bolts, and other strange attachments. All of them required occasional attention. Their presence made me nervous as I took on the task of trying to keep them happy and running.

Even though I had no previous experience with repairing things like a stubborn stove or a dying refrigerator, I was not deterred. With a determination that I would save the money and not pay a pro, I dived into the back of, and under the lid of things and figured out what made them tick or not tick. Before too long I was getting pretty proficient at either fixing an item or at least knowing where to dump it after salvaging a few of its usable spare parts for future repairs.

One of the most memorable adventures I had as a young husband was changing the wax gasket under our rental apartment commode. The morning I walked into the bathroom of our rented apartment and sloshed through about an inch of water in my sock-clad feet, I was committed to finding out where the source of the flow was. To make a short story long, I eventually discovered the leak was at the base of our "throne." I called a friend, and he alerted me to the wax ring that was likely the culprit. Unwilling to wait on the Lord to miraculously heal it and not wanting to pay the price for a plumber, I took my one and only crescent wrench and my lone screwdriver and started on a journey that led me down an exciting road.

As I went along I gathered a few helpful hints. The man at the hardware store where I bought the cheap replacement gasket was especially informative, and with his guidance I went home and hugged the "big white telephone." After removing the bolts that held the commode to the floor I couldn't figure out why it wouldn't lift off. Duh! The water connections had to be detached. One faux pas led to another, but finally I was staring into the disgusting hole in the floor. When I realized I had to use my hands to remove the old gasket, I nearly gagged. The cotton gloves I found did not keep my hands dry but I fought through the nasty mess and got the job done.

To say the least, I learned a lot that day. Never again did I have to ask another soul about how to solve that problem. Fortunately, even though I had handled raw sewage, it was an experience that turned out to be disease free. As the years went by, there were other necessary repair adventures that I encountered. Each one provided new knowledge that has made me a true handyman. I found enjoyment in playing that role even when it spilled over into taking care of our vehicles. While I am not Mr. Goodwrench by any means, I have been able to learn enough to keep a heap rolling down the road.

In regard to my son's bank of knowledge about these things, I confess I have failed to give him sufficient instruction that will benefit him in his future. While I may have inadvertently passed a few ideas on to him, I often took the line of least resistance when it came time to do a repair. Consequently, he rarely observed the process. Most of the time, the reason I didn't involve him was a matter of expediency. While I was doing something crucial like trying to figure out how to replace a water heater element, I was a very focused student. Adding the element of trying to be a teacher to someone in that moment would have been a distraction I admittedly avoided. Once the tedious job was done, I was usually so frustrated with it that the idea of returning to it with my son and giving him a "how to" lesson was an extra mile I didn't care to walk. Consequently, he has reached his young adult years with his "how to fix it" account practically empty. While this blunder may not ultimately have a bearing on the quality of his soul, his lack of repair skills might affect the condition of his house.

I want Nathan to know I am embarrassed that I have failed him in this domestic area. The only good thing that might come of it is that someday the expertise I managed to develop will be a very good excuse to show up at his house and disguise a visit with a repair job.

Communicating

I heard a preacher admit that he considered himself a better "little kid" dad than a "big kid" dad. Somewhere deep inside me his words rang a bell. As I pondered the revelation, I realized it applied to me—especially in the area of my ability to communicate.

From the time my son was a toddler and on into his preadolescent years, I think I was a much better father in terms of talking with him. Why? Because I was as much a kid as he was. I thoroughly enjoyed playing, pretending, and partying with my son. My communication skills were not highly challenged, and I seemed to do well with conveying my simple thoughts. Besides, it doesn't take a "rocket psychologist" to know how to giggle!

Then…he reached the time when his level of intelligence began to reveal an incredibly gifted mind. With an uncanny ability to reason and wrangle with sentences that rivaled the best of scholars, I realized I was being left in the educational dust. In a sense, I was still out on the playground while my son was happily in the classroom.

I know my assessment of those years sounds self-debasing and quite possibly my son would argue that it is not true. If so, he would be kindly saying, "That'll play!" And I would be grateful. However, God has blessed me with a solution to the reality that I am not the most well-stocked treasury where he can withdraw massive amounts of wisdom. To compensate, the Lord in His grace has given me a wife who is beyond brilliant. Annie possesses a wealth of insight and, more importantly, she has a mind that can assess a situation quickly and come up with wisdom that is both godly and accurate in most cases. I stand in awe of her ability to counsel, and Nathan knows I lean heavily on her to provide guidance when I am at a loss for words. How thankful I am that she fills in the gap that I candidly admit exists. Nathan should feel honored that she is on our team.

The Birdies

Golfers would agree that hardly anything is nicer than seeing a few numbers on the scorecard that have circles around them. Or, if you're a pro who is walking a course during a tournament, you'd look for the numbers in red that have been mounted on the scoreboard. The meaning of either is a cause for joy. It indicates that the hole was completed subpar. (For those who aren't hackers, "subpar" is a good thing!)

As a dad, I have garnered a few circles in my day. One of my very favorite birdies happened on hole 9 at a course near our house. The green was elevated and about 150 yards away. It sat next to the clubhouse, and my main concern on the tee was not to bean anybody who might have been standing 150 yards to the right of the flag at the concession stand.

I took the best aim I could and followed through as best I knew how. The eight iron pinged when I struck the ball, and it sounded pretty good. The white sphere shrunk in size as I watched it sail to the top of the hill and out of sight. I hoped it had landed on the green but assumed the ball rolled off the other side. When our threesome got to the putting surface I was utterly amazed to find my ball waiting for me about three inches from the cup. My heart pounded as I walked over, removed the flagstick, and carefully tapped in. The imaginary gallery roared. It was a red-number day for me!

That birdie is a good illustration of what fatherhood is like for most of us. When it comes to rightly raising a child, we line up our shots the best we know how. We try with all that is in us to remember all the correct moves to make as the club face is taken back. We attempt to keep both feet on the ground when the ball is struck, and we try not to gloat when we think we at least hit the fairway. While we hope all things were done well, we really can't know at the moment. Instead, we have to gather up our things and, with faith in the Lord that He has blessed our efforts, walk ahead through time for a distance. Sometimes a lot of the calendar pages have to be turned before we know whether or not we're still in bounds. Here are a few of my "father shots" that have yielded some birdies:

The Fear of God

When I was around six years old, I vividly recall being in a room with my mother and one of her friends. They were talking as I played. I don't remember what they were saying, but I do recall the tone of their voices. It was low and intense, as if they were sharing something scary. While I might have appeared unaware of their serious conversation, I remember being drawn to the sound of their voices. Suddenly, as if all other noises in the universe stopped in respectful silence for the words that were about to be said, my mother delivered a sentence that rang in my young ears as clear as a bell. To this very day, it continues to echo in my head.

She raised her eyebrows and slowly moved her head to one side. Her statement started with a melodic, alto tone and finished with a dramatic rise and fall: "Oh! My! I do fear the Lord!"

I froze when I heard her speak. I couldn't believe my ears. I suppose it was the usage of the words "fear" and "Lord" in the same sentence that got my attention. I had never heard anyone—especially my mother—say such a thing. I was unwilling to ask her what she meant by it for fear of the answer.

Until that moment when I heard my mother say that she was so afraid of Him, God had been a true source of comfort for me. Innocent mealtime and bedtime prayers, Christmas joy, Easter celebrations, and happy songs about God in church had been all I had ever known about Him. Then all of a sudden the number-one adult woman in my life who cared so deeply for me announces she was terrified of this God. I was confused.

Because she probably didn't mean for her words to find my ears, there was no way she could have known what turmoil I went through for the next several weeks. I struggled with things like going to sleep with the light off and being outside alone. I resolved to wait for the lightning to turn us all into smoke. I, too, had become afraid of *Him.*

As it turned out, my mother's honest expression of her fear of the Lord became an incorruptible seed that found the good soil of my heart. Eventually, it bore the best of fruit. I finally learned that her meaning of "having a fear of God" was very biblical in that she had a deep, abiding respect for the eternal, matchless, wise, one-and-only true God. I also discovered that she stood on very solid ground when it came to embracing such a level of reverence. The Scripture supports her holy fear. For example,

> Praise the LORD! How blessed is the man who fears [reveres] the LORD… (Psalm 112:1).
>
> LORD, I have heard the report about You and I fear… (Habakkuk 3:2).
>
> You shall revere your God; I am the LORD (Leviticus 19:14).

As a result of having seen my mother's (as well as my dad's) attitude about the importance of showing a healthy respect for God's awesomeness, not a single day has passed since that evening that I have not remembered that God is great. In one way or another, especially when sin entered the picture, in each 24-hour period that I have lived, the fear of God has returned to my heart. With a sincere hope that I could pass on this kind of reverence, I sought ways to teach it to my children.

When the kids began to show their ability to reason, I wasted no time in challenging them to understand God's incredible power and the purity of His unequaled character. One of the first things I did was to introduce them to the truth recorded in Isaiah 43:10:

> "You are My witnesses," declares the Lord, "and My servant whom I have chosen, so that you may know and understand that I am He. Before Me there was no God formed, and there will be none after Me."

I loved to watch their little faces begin to scrunch up in mental anguish as they tried to imagine how it was that God had no beginning and has no end and that He is not subject to the limits of time. I could almost see the smoke coming out of their ears as their brains would bend and grind in an effort to either go back beyond the boundary of the first minute on the "big clock" or go forward past the last minute. Knowing they were totally incapable of imagining that God has no beginning or no ending, I would continue to urge them to try with, "Keep going back, back, back…forward, forward, forward." I couldn't help but smile when their eyes would close tightly as they tried to journey to a place the human mind cannot go.

Finally, they would sigh, throw their heads back, and give up. That was my cue to remind them that the very God they couldn't fully comprehend with their noggins of flesh is the same one whose greatness demands that we never cease to show Him the utmost respect. Or, as my mother would put it, they could say, "Oh! My! I do fear the Lord!" I am grateful to report that my son, who loved to take part in those mind-boggling exercises in mental futility so many years ago, has grown to appreciate God's unfathomable greatness.

One other means I used to instill an ongoing reverence for our heavenly Father was to help Nathan understand that *self-respect* is permissible and even encouraged in the Scriptures. Self-esteem, however, was the original problem in the Garden of Eden. I want him to accept the well-known Psalm 139 passage that reminds us that we are "fearfully and wonderfully made" as a God-given go-ahead for humans to show ourselves a sufficient amount of respect. The purpose of knowing that it was He who formed our intricate, inward parts and wove us in our mothers' wombs is that we would see His incredible, creative power. The miracle of life should be one of the things that inspires us to adore our Creator. It's only when our worship turns inward and amazement is focused on that which is created that we get into some serious trouble.

I want my son to know that it was on the day when the first sin was committed in the Garden of Eden that humanity began to drift away from fellowship with God. That was the day when Satan, the enemy of our souls, began his attempts to replace self-respect with self-esteem. As Adam and Eve began to naval gaze, their attention was shifted from who made them to what He had made. Essentially, man and woman became idols unto themselves.

The 60s and 70s gave us the "me generation," and by the time Nathan came along, the vicious waves of that God-forgetting mentality were still washing over America. (Really, has there ever not been a "me generation" since the Garden of Eden?) Through the years, however, I continued to remind my son that no one on this planet who is or ever has been will be permitted to sit on God's throne. It is reserved for Him—

and Him alone. "The LORD is in His holy temple; the LORD's throne is in heaven" (Psalm 11:4).

One of my most favorite ways to help Nathan (and others) remember God's majesty was with a T-shirt and a baseball cap. I'm not necessarily a big fan of putting the timeless truths of the Bible onto rags of clothing, but when the message serves to challenge errant worldviews, I have been known to get in line to purchase it. Nathan wore the shirt and I sported the hat. Both of them had this quip: "There is a God, and you're not Him!" This generated many comments and effectively witnessed to the people around us. It was especially delightful when one or both of us would be wearing our "billboard" onto an airplane. Many of the passengers already seated would take in the silent sermon as we shuffled past them in the aisle, and if someone reacted it was never lukewarm. They would either sneer in disgust or smile and say something like, "Amen, Brother!"

I am convinced that instilling the fear of God in our children is the one attitude that will serve them best throughout their lives. It will affect everything they do, everything they think, and everything they become. If assisting Nathan in giving his highest esteem to God alone is the only parental birdie I ever get on the course of this life, it is, by far, the most important one I could circle on the scorecard.

Respect for Elders

Prior to our first pregnancy, Annie and I got to know a couple in the Nashville area whose children won the blue ribbon in the best-behaved category. The one thing about them that generated such a high regard in our minds was their consistent and careful attention to the usage of "yes, ma'am" and "yes, sir."

It almost felt awkward to be referred to with such respect from kids who were so young. It was also very uncommon to hear. It was obvious that they were very well trained in the art of courtesy. Annie and I found ourselves literally wanting to be around those children. Because they so impressed us with their polite demeanor, we determined that if we ever had children, they would learn the same manners.

Moving forward in time about five years... By then we had a three-year-old and one on the way. As early as we could start, we began coaching them in the graceful habit of properly addressing anyone who was either obviously well beyond them in years or who was significantly taller.

I loved to watch teenagers look in shock at our little kids when they spoke to their "seniors" with "yes, sir," and "yes, ma'am." Some of them even tried to convince our youngsters that they shouldn't do such a thing. However, Nathan and Heidi were not deterred. They diligently used the prescribed verbiage.

As a result of their faithfulness to show honor to their elders, they discovered that their investment of respect had a noticeable return. They found that those who were older treated them with the same dignity they had offered. This "social gain" put them ahead of the game of life in some very real ways. For example, they were more apt to be called on to be leaders because their simple "yes, ma'ams" and "yes, sirs" made them sound more mature. While I was quite proud of their advanced demeanor, I believe their willingness to not only understand this kind of courtesy, but to be cooperative in it, was born out of the reverence that had been instilled in them for God.

While I admit that I relentlessly demanded this kind of behavior from my kids, I did realize that they needed an occasional emotional break from such a rigid requirement. As a form of "release" for them, so that their old dad would not be seen as a total bore, I did allow a little humorous game to be played from time to time. I'm not sure how it developed but it was fun when I'd say to them, "Nathan and Heidi, are you going to say 'yes ma'am' and 'yes, sir' today?"

With a smile of permitted mischief on their faces, both of them would answer with a loud, "Yep!" We would always chuckle at their response, and they seemed to somehow feel a certain, momentary relief from the rigors of proper etiquette. Though I was never sure if joking with them in such a way was a good thing to do, it didn't seem to harm their character. To this day, they currently still engage in the appropriate usage of their mannerly responses to their elders. This, too, is a birdie!

Tithing

Since it is true that God has supplied all our needs according to His riches (see Philippians 4:19), to give a healthy percentage of it back to Him is the best way to recognize that all we have comes from His hand. I have no doubt that this truth made it to my son's heart because of what happened recently. He reported to me that he had prayed that the Lord would somehow supply an extra $500 to cover an unanticipated expense. Excitedly he announced that the very amount he needed came in from some unexpected sources...plus $50! I was beaming with joy when he realized, "God even supplied the tithe!"

Tithing includes cash, of course, but I also wanted my son to know that we are free to give other gifts such as time and labor. I have seen him respond to this message as well. He has done everything from mowing countless acres of grass to producing a mountain of recordings for friends in need.

Priorities

If you have more than three priorities, you have none at all. In an attempt to help my son not spread himself too thin in terms of his responsibilities, I often reminded him of this statement. I heard it years ago, and it was one of the most life-changing thoughts that has ever been presented to me. I began to reconsider which of my roles in life were the most important. After prayerful assessment, I determined that my walk with Christ was first on the list. Because of the eternal implications of this relationship, I couldn't ignore it. Being a husband and a father were next on the list. Adapting the wisdom found in Luke 9:25, I would often whisper to myself: "For what is a man profited if he gains the whole world, and loses [his family]?"

My unyielding commitment to Annie and our children resulted in some very unpopular choices in terms of our relationships in the business world. Though Annie's and my work in a Christian music ministry was my third priority, Nathan watched and listened as I said "no" to some very good opportunities that came along. While they might have significantly advanced our career, to have accepted them might have hindered our family's time for togetherness. For that reason, there were "Steve and Annie Chapman as musicians" decisions, and "mom and dad" decisions.

I discovered early on that my son was getting this message when, at around the age of nine, he told us that he wanted to be a policeman. He added to his announcement the following mandate, "Of course, my kids will ride with me in the backseat of the car." I trust that the seed of devotion to his family will yield good fruit in years to come!

So ends my list of bogeys and birdies. If by candidly showing my scorecard I have encouraged you in your fatherhood endeavors, keep in mind that God has plenty of grace to cover things like divots, lost balls, and even thrown clubs. He is a kind Father who understands our desire to get better at the game. For those of us who have already completed our walk on the fairways of parenthood and who wait on the balcony of the clubhouse, may God hear our prayers while we watch and pray for our sons who are still out on the course playing their rounds!

10

Little Sayings
with a Lot of Truth

In many words there is emptiness.

ECCLESIASTES 5:7

God seems to appreciate sincerity that is seasoned with brevity. Think of how much was said, for example with, "It is finished." The crucified Christ needed no long, drawn-out discourse to explain His victory on the cross. Three simple words equaled a universe of meaning. I want my son to know that he can often find an orchard of wisdom in the tiny seed of a sentence.

I have always been a big fan of little sayings. I love the way that so much truth can be packed into such a small space. Perhaps this is a trait peculiar to men, one that is divinely wired into our psyches, a characteristic that allows us to respond best to short phrases that are long on information. This being quite possible, it might explain how men can exchange volumes of data in flash-card fashion.

One comedian certainly understood this male characteristic. He offered a recount of a conversation between two "good ol' Southern boys" who were talking about going to lunch together. It went something like this:

"Howdy"
"Hey"
"Doin' awrite?"
"Yep...you?
"Fine...J'eat yet?"
"Naw, joo?"
"Naw"
"Ywan-to?"
"Yep!"

And off they went to burger row to share even deeper from their hearts.

I realize that not all men are as economical with their words as the two fellows in the above dialogue. However, it could have easily been me and any one of my buddies that supplied the comic with the idea for the bit. I am often guilty of attempting to reduce an entire text to a fortune cookie-sized comment. For some reason, I find it exhilarating. (After all, my main vocation for many years has been songwriting, the art of squeezing a lifetime of experience into a three-minute musical.)

What's so amazing about certain quips that I have encountered is how a spark of words can ignite a forest fire of change in my heart. Through the years, there have been a handful of proverbs that have altered the course of my life. And, just as important, many of the little pieces of wisdom turned out to be the missing part of the "what do I do now" puzzle that I was so desperately trying to complete.

I want my son to know about some of these sayings. To leave them embedded in my soul and not pass them on would be a great disservice. He will likely garner several of his own as he lives, but I want him to have these to add to his collection. I offer some of them along with my best recollection of their origin, a passage of Scripture that reveals the biblical aspect (if appropriate), and a comment or two about how they influenced my life. Others are self-explanatory. It is my hope that at least one, if not a few of them, will be useful in guiding Nathan's steps toward a closer relationship with God and a walk of integrity with those who journey next to him.

Sayings from Family Members

"Partly cloudy, partly clear."
Ewing H. Steele, 1895–1994

I sat quietly with my Grandfather Steele on the front porch of his house in West Virginia. His 90-year-old frame was parked comfortably in the chair he had used for years to monitor the street where he lived. As men often do, we were keeping our thoughts to ourselves. Suddenly he broke the silence with "partly cloudy, partly clear." Then he was quiet again.

I have not only cherished his statement since, but I frequently repeat it. What I heard him say was the sentiment of a man who understood Paul's admission in Philippians 4:11: "Not that I speak from want, for I have learned to be content in whatever circumstances I am."

Paul is commended for his attitude because we know of the great struggles he encountered in following Christ. Being shipwrecked and jailed, for example, didn't deter him. He pressed diligently onward. But Paul's was not the only name on the list of those who have had their share of trials. My grandpa knew some hard times, too. The coal mines had provided plenty of trouble. Missing fingers, a broken and replaced hip, and worst of all, the "Black Lung" disease that wracked his body. Furthermore, he, along with my Grandma Steele, raised 11 wonderful children. That, too, offered sufficient challenges. Still, he ran the race of life faithfully. Through it all he was able to appreciate both the clouds of life as well as the sunshine. Somehow, he was able to see them both at the same time as precious to behold. I want to be like him

"No matter how poor you get, you don't have to be nasty!"
Maude Steele, 1900–1970

My Grandmother Steele birthed 12 children. One of them went to be with the Lord soon after being born, but the rest of the kids filled their small home in West Virginia. Though their funds and space were always limited, she would not allow her dwelling to become a victim of clutter and filth. As far as she was concerned, her home was a reflection of her heart. It may have been simple and crowded, but it was always spotless, even in the unseen parts of the back rooms.

I never really understood my own mother's approach to "deep cleaning" until I realized how she had been raised. When I was growing up, springtime would come and my mama would have me dusting in the oddest of places. For example, a washcloth wrapped tightly around the end of a flat, wooden yardstick served as a tool to reach far under the refrigerator to gather the accumulated dust from underneath it. "No one ever looks under here, Mom!" would be my argument as I reluctantly obeyed. Her response was intuitive, "Yes, I realize that, Son. But *I* know the dirt is there. It bothers *me*, and it has to go!"

My grandma's zeal for cleanliness to the core, which she passed on to my mother, reminds me of the probing truth of Psalm 90:8: "You have placed our iniquities before You, our secret sins in the light of Your presence." The "clean beneath the surface" attitude eventually had an impact on my life that was more than physical. Much later, I wrote the following lyric.

The Secret Place

My heart is like a house
One day I let the Savior in
And there are many rooms
Where we would visit now and then
But then one day He saw that door
I knew the day had come too soon
I said, "Jesus, I'm not ready
For us to visit in that room."

'Cause that's a place in my heart
Where even I don't go
I had some things hidden there
I don't want no one to know
But He handed me the key
With tears of love on His face
He said, "I want to make you clean
Let Me go in your secret place."

So I opened up the door
And as the two of us walked in
I was so ashamed
His light revealed my hidden sin
But when I think about that room now
I'm not afraid anymore
'Cause I know my hidden sin
No longer hides behind that door

That was a place in my heart
Where even I wouldn't go
I had some things hidden there

I didn't want no one to know
But He handed me the key
With tears of love on His face
He made me clean
I let Him in my secret place.
Is there a place in your heart
Where even you don't go?[16]

"Throw your feet out and be a good horse."

George S. Chapman, 1893–1975

These words of encouragement came from the heart of my industrious, hard-working Grandpa Chapman. More than once I, along with his 11 children and a yard full of grandkids, heard him lift his voice and call out this phrase as he raised his left arm in the air to accent their delivery. He longed for all of his loved ones to rise above their own handicaps (a word he never used) and excel at whatever they endeavored.

His reference to the way a well-disciplined horse would powerfully lift its feet and plow through the mud-laden hillsides of West Virginia was a vivid picture of determination. He had not allowed the shotgun blast that destroyed his right arm when he was eight years old to steal the quality of his life. Instead, he pressed through the loss and managed to become a successful teacher, principal, school-board member, a highway construction superintendent, and, eventually, one of Logan County's most respected businessmen. I am proud to be one of his kin. To have known him makes my feet feel light, even when life gets heavy. With him in mind, I often recall, "I press on toward the goal for the prize of the upward call of God in Christ Jesus" (Philippians 3:14).

"Want a sandwich?"

Easter Chapman, 1900–1985

While the three words "I love you" might be worthy rivals for the thing most grandkids enjoy hearing most from a grandma, "Want a sandwich?" could easily win the contest for me. Grandma Chapman somehow knew that love was best realized when it tasted like something good. There was nothing more affectionate than two slices of white bread that held a thick, round chunk of fresh bologna, "real" mayonnaise, and a juicy cut of a ripe, handpicked, homegrown tomato. It makes me drool just to remember it.

What I saw in my Grandma Chapman's character was that of a true servant. She willingly embraced the admonition found in Philippians 2:3,4: "Do nothing from selfishness or empty conceit, but with humility of mind regard one another as more important than yourselves; do not merely look out for your own personal interests, but also for the interests of others." Not a soul that knew her would disagree that she indeed understood the attitude of Christ. Grandma Chapman was a woman worth following...especially to her kitchen!

"Take my boots off."

N.R. Williamson, 1920–1998

These were the last words of Annie's dad as he passed away. He had battled the damaging effects of a major heart attack that struck him when he was 51 years old. For nearly 30 years he farmed with a heart that was 80 percent damaged. Knowing he was susceptible to another attack at any given moment didn't stop him from living.

On the day he went to be with the Lord, he had been out tending some calves. When his heart began to race and he sensed the danger he was in, he forced through the pain and made his way to the house. Instead of dialing 911, though, he called a neighbor and asked her to help him secure the gate he feared he had left open. She heard his labored breathing and rushed to his side. As she assisted him, he inquired about the cattle gate. Satisfied that all was secure, he then asked her to remove his boots.

None of us are totally sure what he was thinking in that moment. Perhaps it was as simple as feeling his feet were numbed by the cold and needed warming. Or, because of the barnyard mud on his shoes, his respect for the house-care wishes of his sweetheart who had preceded him in passing two years earlier might have been on his mind.

For whatever reason he said them, his last words will never be forgotten. Most of us have chosen to accept them as a farmer's paraphrase of 2 Timothy 4:7: "I have fought the good fight, I have finished the course, I have kept the faith." Because we loved him so much and miss him today, we find great comfort in the thought that comes only two verses later in that chapter that we're sure N.R. would have us notice: "Make every effort to come to me soon." We interpret this as, "Do what you must to maintain a walk with Christ. If you do, I'll see you after awhile."

"I will not go to hell over a dollar!"
Sylvia Williamson, 1921–1996

Annie's mother was one of my most favorite human beings who ever set foot on this planet. Her dignity was graced with a sense of humor that kept her children, grandchildren, and in-laws glued to each moment we spent with her. In addition, Sylvia had an affection for honesty that displayed an obviously God-fearing heart. Her "hell over a dollar" statement has been used often by the Lord to probe at me in the way a shepherd uses his staff to lead a lamb away from danger.

The story behind Sylvia's often-repeated words came about after her brother, Raymond, had died. While cleaning his attic, a laundry basket full of cash was found. There were large bills rolled up into tight bundles. Some elderly, hermit-type neighbors had asked him to keep their accumulation of Social Security income in his possession. Since the neighbors and Raymond were now dead, what to do with the money was a hot topic. Unwilling to confiscate the thousands of dollars and secretly pocket the money, Annie's mom and her sisters returned every penny to the source—the state of West Virginia.

Some folks thought she was silly for giving up such a wad of cash; however, she felt that the funds belonged to the people of her state. One skeptic remarked, "Somebody at the courthouse will put that basket in the trunk of his car and the state will never see it." Sylvia's response? "That's their business. Mine is to do the right thing. I will not go to hell over a dollar!" Believing that "the love of money is a root of all sorts of evil" (1 Timothy 6:10), she gave up the riches she could have had. Her desire was that of the writer of Hebrews 13:18: "Pray for us, for we are sure that we have a good conscience, desiring to conduct ourselves honorably in all things." Sylvia's unyielding determination to do the right thing was a product of believing this absolute truth: There is no softer pillow than a conscience that is clear!

"Be grateful for criticism. It'll keep the woe off of you."

P.J. Chapman

This wisdom came from the understanding heart of the second best man who ever put on the garment of flesh. The first was Christ, the next is my dad. Among the many life-guiding insights he passed on to me, this is one of my favorites. It came at a time when I was wrestling with the consequences of writing song lyrics that didn't fit into the mold of commercialism. The record company I was with was encouraging me to forsake the "hard" subjects of life and pen some songs that would be more acceptable for radio airplay. In addition, my willingness to sing heart-probing lyrics in public settings was garnering a few challenging reactions. When I alerted my dad to my struggle with whether or not to "back off" from what I felt God was calling me to do, he took me to Luke 6:26: "Woe to you when all men speak well of you."

With comforting confidence he assured me that if I was convinced I was doing the will of God by tackling the tough issues of life through songs, then the criticism could be viewed as confirmation that the devil didn't care for the good that would result in people's lives. He also stated that as far as public performance goes, when the Holy Spirit is free to move, the listeners will be truly entertained—even as they are being deeply challenged.

To yield to the wishes of the market-minded executives and write only the lighter lyrics, would have meant stepping out from under the flow of God's approval for my work. With Dad's encouraging wisdom, I stayed the course. Even though I seriously displeased a few folks, I don't regret my decision because I avoided the woe that follows spiritual compromise.

"If you see he'll die a sinner, go ahead and take him right now. In Jesus' name, amen."
Lillian Chapman

If you went to the dictionary and looked up the word "tenacious," you would find my mother's name next to it. It took a ton of nerve to pray the prayer just quoted. Though it was risky, she lifted this courageous petition to God in my presence somewhere in the midst of my thirteenth year.

I'm not sure what I might have been doing to cause her to pray so seriously, but my behavior must have been terribly disturbing. At any rate, she came into my bedroom one morning and dropped to her knees next to my bed, grabbed my right forearm with both of her hands, and looked straight up to heaven. Then she proceeded to put my very life on the line.

After she said "amen," I gulped in fear and waited for the lightning to strike. I had watched God answer her prayers, sometimes within minutes. I assumed I was about to be smoke. Yet I'm still around to this day. *Whew!*

What would make a woman as sweet as my beloved mother offer this kind of prayer for her son? The answer is simple. She knew the worst thing for me was not that I would fail to graduate from high school, not go to college, not get a good job, not marry the right person, or not get a deadly disease. As bad as all those things might be, the worst thing would be that I would die without knowing Christ and allowing Him to be Lord of my life. She knew that without salvation through Jesus alone, my soul would be forever lost in its sad separation from God. That would be the worst fate of all.

It was for that reason she prayed in such an unusual way. Needless to say, my mother's cry to God altered the course of my life. I will be eternally grateful that she was fiercely unwilling to allow the enemy of the souls of her children to cause them to be among the unfortunate number mentioned in Matthew 13:40-42: "So just as the tares are gathered up and burned with fire, so shall it be at the end of the age. The Son of Man will send forth His angels, and they will gather out of His kingdom all stumbling blocks, and those who commit lawlessness, and will throw them into the furnace of fire; in that place there will be weeping and gnashing of teeth."

With a resolve to allow God to do what He must to assure her that I would be saved from such a fiery fate, my mother prayed in faith. She did so trusting that I would be among the number spoken of in verse 43 of the same passage: "Then the righteous will shine forth as the sun in the kingdom of their Father." What a great blessing to have been born to a woman like my mother!

"God is the audience!"

Jeannie Martin

My sister is a skilled and anointed musician and worship leader at the church that she and her husband, Gene, pastor in Ohio. Before she plays a note or sings a lyric at the opening of a service, she often reminds the congregation that, like many other things in God's kingdom that are completely opposite of this world, there is something totally unique about the activity of worship. Here on the earth when a singer sings, he or she normally stands as the celebrated individual on the stage and performs for those who fill the seats in the room. However, in the divine setting, the audience becomes the performer and the stage is reserved for the one who listens. If the stage is the place of honor, God alone belongs on it. And when the saints play the last note on their instruments and their voices fall silent in the building, they should find joy in the sound of applause, not the cheers of ovation that extol human talents, but the quiet applause heard deep in the heart that comes from only one pair of nail-scarred hands.

"Courage is not the absence of fear, it is proceeding in the face of it."

Annie Chapman

This maxim, saturated with truth, echoes in the life of my son's mother, who, I am happy to say, is my wife. Like pure gold, the value in this wisdom is priceless, especially when understood how brave she had to be as she dealt with the devastating effects of being raped when she was a child. Satan attempted to destroy her life by working through the deviant actions of a hired farmhand when she was merely five years old. The anger and rage that ensued was debilitating physically and spiritually. Yet she fought through it and, with the courage that comes only from our kind heavenly Father, the war for her soul was won. She is now the sweetest, most lovable person I know. To say that she understands the need for fearlessness through faith is an understatement. I'll be forever grateful to have been called to walk beside her in marriage.

"You don't understand, Mommy, Jesus glows in the dark!"

Heidi Chapman Beall

This profound statement was made around Christmastime in 1985. After tearing through several layers of Scotch tape, Annie finally got down to the small Christmas gift our daughter, Heidi, had given to her. It was a very small, plastic nativity. As Annie held the little Joseph, Mary, and baby Jesus, she tenderly said, "Thank you, Heidi," and started to go about her business. Heidi could tell that her mother had missed the most important feature of the set. In turn, Annie could see that her little girl looked a little disappointed. That's when Heidi offered the unforgettable report that "Jesus glows in the dark." Annie's heart melted when she realized what a wonderful symbol was found in the small, plastic trinket. What other kind of Savior would we want than the one who shines in the midst of our sin-darkened culture? It is He who said, "I am the Light of the world" (John 8:12).

"What's wrong with being right!"

Jeannie Martin

This quip from my sister is perhaps the most profound truth that can be offered to those who may feel they have short-changed the world of evangelism by not having a "juicy testimony." This comforting thought came to her one day when she was musing on the fact that she had been born into a Christian home, never severely strayed from the path of holiness (except for beating me up a time or two when we were younger!), and has journeyed through her years without personal scandal and without bringing reproach on the name of Christ.

Though she knew her "walk" had been steady, she began to feel that her life had been less than spectacular. She was feeling concerned that by having, for example, no drugs, alcohol, murder, jail time, or self-inflicted social diseases in her history her declaration of God's ability to change a life might not be as strong as others. As she wallowed in her fears, suddenly a still, small voice whispered in the ear of her heart, "There's nothing wrong with being right."

In her spirit, my sister was convinced that God had spoken His approval of her choice to carefully stay on "the narrow path." His kind assurance was all that was needed. Once again she was at peace. From that day forward, she repeated those words of wisdom time and again to her three children who have turned out wonderfully.

As an added note to this thought, I want my son to know that when a person manages to snatch his normal Christian life from the jaws of sensationalism, a tremendous advantage is gained. A picture of that reward is found in the life of the prodigal son's brother as recorded in Luke 15. Though we're not told the reason, it is very clear that he showed some serious anger and jealousy for the "party" that the jubilant father threw for his sibling who had returned from a world of sin and hopelessness. While some would insist that he became irreparably bitter over the deference shown to the prodigal, I contend that the fire of jealousy was quickly doused by his wise father's words in verse 31: "And he [the father] said to him [the prodigal's brother], 'Son, you have always been with me, and all that is mine is yours.'"

The implication seems to be that because of how the wayward boy had squandered his share of the estate, he could not be fully trusted with the father's wealth. I can't help but believe that the brother who had stayed at home did not receive his father's words as a rebuke, but as an incredible, humbling compliment to his trustworthiness.

With his father's recognition of such consistent devotion, I believe a heart in turmoil was calmed. I can only imagine that from that day on, he willingly remained faithful to his father's name.

Based on the premise that unwavering, reliable righteousness is a virtue that deserves great honor, my sweet sister would be qualified to ask any pilgrim who feels undervalued because they think their testimony lacks the high drama: "What's wrong with being right?"

"God bless those who give, bless those who don't have to give, and have mercy on those who have it, but won't give it!"

P.J. Chapman

This was my dad's offertory prayer on a Sunday morning. I remember it nearly every time the plate is passed at church

Memorable Sayings from Others

"True success is ending up in heaven."
Bumper sticker

**"It is a tragedy to be a public success
and a private failure."**
Gordon MacDonald

"An unguarded strength is a double weakness."
Oswald Chambers

**"Better to want what you don't have
than to have what you don't want."**
Author unknown

**"When we're young we spend our health
getting wealth and when we are old we spend
our wealth getting health."**
Mike Murdoch

**"Don't criticize someone until you've walked
a mile in their shoes...that way if they get
mad at you, you'll already be a mile away!"**
Author unknown

**"Don't think about their wallets. You have to think
about their hearts. That's where the 'change' needs to be."**
Bob Hughey

This unforgettable advice came on the heels of Bob's agree-
ment to provide ongoing counsel to a music group I was a part

of during the mid 1970s. We had asked him, along with John Acuff and Larry Napier, to oversee our work as Christian musicians. He said he would do so only if we resolved to operate debt free. Bob's godly guidance is still pertinent!

"Whatever you do as a husband, make sure your wife is happy first."
Archie Boone

Some of the best advice I could have ever received as a new husband.

"If you're leaving, I'm going with you."
Anonymous

A husband in North Carolina said this to his wife in their tenth year of marriage. He coined this phrase after they had a big fight and she was angrily packing a suitcase to leave him. As he began to pack his own bag, she asked, "What are you doing?" That's when he verbalized perhaps this most poignant example of commitment I have ever heard.

"Character is what you are when no one's looking."
Author unknown

So much said in so few words. I love it! This quip reverberates in my heart and is often followed by: If I suddenly died, what would my family find when they went through my truck, workshop, chest of drawers, attic, or any other place they could find evidence of my behavior? Is there anything I would dread for them to discover? To live so that no residue of willful sin is hidden among my belongings is a challenging goal.

In light of such a high objective, all of us would do well to be like the young man whose dad offered to mow a yard for him that he had promised another person he would do. Because he had some other errands he needed to do, the young fellow took his dad up on the offer. As the son was driving across town he realized he had misplaced the mower key in the course of moving to his new apartment. He quickly called his dad on the cell phone, and said, "Dad, I'm so glad you haven't left the house yet because I just remembered that I'm not sure where the key to the mower is. It's somewhere in my stuff. Please feel free to go to my apartment and look through everything."

As the dad was perusing through his son's belongings, it suddenly occurred to him that his boy must have undoubtedly been living a life of righteousness because no one would allow another person to search through their possessions if there was something they didn't want found. How grateful the father was for a son who had nothing to hide. The dad in this story, by the way, is me.

"Pray that I will not entertain one wayward thought."

James Dobson

I heard Dr. Dobson respond to a group of men who had asked him how they could pray for him. Knowing the enormity of the cost of maintaining an organization like Focus on the Family, I assumed his answer would involve monetary or material need. Instead, his single request for prayer support had to do with the maintenance of the integrity of his heart. I was moved that day to always give the same answer when asked how others could pray for me.

"A worker's appetite works for him, for his hunger urges him on."

Proverbs 16:26

While this quote is wisdom for the laborer, it is also a concept that an employer should remember. Annie reminded me of this passage when I made the mistake of prepaying a less-than-credible carpenter. He never did return to finish the job. I learned a big lesson about how *not* to do business.

"Seek the Giver, not the gift."

Vep Ellis

As a young Christian surrounded by a community of believers who were enthralled by the Charismatic movement of the day and sincerely seeking the "gifts of the Spirit," Vep Ellis' admonition was very timely. It turned my focus from the miracles to the source—Christ Jesus.

"It will cost you nothing to tell a lost soul about Jesus. It will cost them everything if they don't hear your message!"

Author unknown

Last Words

But God, being rich in mercy, because of His great love with which He loved us, even when we were dead in our transgressions, made us alive together with Christ (by grace you have been saved), and raised us up with Him, and seated us with Him in the heavenly places in Christ Jesus, so that in the ages to come He might show the surpassing riches of His grace in kindness toward us in Christ Jesus.

EPHESIANS 2:4-7

I have often wondered what I would say if I knew I had just a few minutes to live and was given the opportunity to talk to my family in those fleeting moments. I am confident I would not speak about possessions gained or lost, dreams realized or unfulfilled, successful or not so successful exploits, or any other thing temporal. The last saying I would want to utter echoes the apostle Paul's words found in Philippians 2:21: "To live is Christ, to die is gain."

These are the things I want my son to know.

Notes

1. Steve Chapman/1981/Dawn Treader Music SESAC/Shepherds Fold Music/ BMI. All rights reserved. Used by permission. Administered by EMI Christian Music Pub.

2. Steve Chapman/Times and Seasons Music/BMI/1995. Used by permission.

3. Steve Chapman/Times and Seasons Music/BMI/1988. Used by permission.

4. Nathan Chapman, "The Brother/Sister Song"/Times and Seasons Music/ BMI/1988. Used by permission.

5. Nathan Chapman/Times and Seasons Music/BMI/1997. Used by permission.

6. Steve Chapman/Times and Seasons Music/BMI/1995. Used by permission.

7. Stephanie Schlosser Chapman/Times and Seasons Music/BMI/2000.

8. Steve Chapman/Times and Seasons Music/BMI/1980. Used by permission.

9. Steve and Annie Chapman—words/Steve Chapman—music. Dawn Treader Music/SESAC & Shepherds Fold Music BMI/1987. All rights reserved/used by permission/admin. by EMI Christian Music.

10. Steve Chapman/Times and Seasons Music/BMI/1995. Used by permission.

11. Steve Chapman/Shepherds Fold Music/BMI/1986. Used by permission.

12. Steve Chapman/Times and Seasons Music/BMI/1999. Used by permission.

13. Steve Chapman/Times and Seasons Music/BMI/1998. Used by permission.

14. Steve Chapman/Times and Seasons Music/BMI/1998. Used by permission.

15. Steve Chapman/Word Spring Music, Inc./1978. Used by permission.

16. Steve Chapman/Shepherds Fold Music/BMI/1981. All rights reserved/used by permission/admin. by EMI Christian Music Pub.

About the Author

Proudly claiming West Virginia as his home state, Steve Chapman grew up as the son of a preacher. He met his wife, Annie, in junior high school in 1963. In March of 1975, they married after dating a few months and settled in Nashville, Tennessee. There they have raised their son and daughter, Nathan and Heidi.

Steve is president of S&A Family, Inc., an organization formed to oversee the production of the Chapman's recorded music. They have had "family life" as the theme of their lyrics since they began singing together in 1980. As Dove Award-winning artists, their schedule sends them to over 100 cities a year to present concerts that feature songs from over 15 recorded projects.

Steve's love of hunting began in his early teens on a weekend when one of his dad's church members invited him to tag along on an October squirrel hunt. Archery is his first choice for use in the field, followed by muzzle loader, and then pistol or rifle. To date, according to Steve's calculations, he has entered the woods before daylight on at least a thousand mornings. He says he hopes for just as many more.

As a member of API's pro-staff team, Steve uses and endorses API treestands.

Other Books by the Chapmans

A Look at Life from a Deer Stand
Steve Chapman

Taking you on his successful and not-so-successful hunts, Chapman reveals the skills for successful hunting—and living. With excitement and humor, he shares the parallels between hunting and walking with God.

A Hunter Sets His Sights
Steve Chapman

Bursting with enthusiasm, Steve shares challenging quests for game and life-changing encounters with God. From hunting whitetails to encountering bull elks, you'll experience the adrenaline-pumping action and meditative moments experienced in God's great outdoors.

With God on a Deer Hunt
Steve Chapman

Capturing the excitement of matching wits with the elusive whitetail, Steve invites you to join him in the breathtaking joy of entering God's presence. You'll encounter the quiet wisdom and often humorous adventures that accompany the pursuit of big game and discover insights into hunting and spiritual growth.

Good Husband's Guide to Balancing Hobbies
Steve Chapman

Avid hunter Steve Chapman enthusiastically pursues a lifelong hobby while remaining passionate about his wife and home. Knowing the perils of spending too much time in the woods, he prayed, studied God's Word, and sought advice. The result? Nine life–changing principles to balancing hobbies and marriage.

A Woman's Answer to Anger
Annie Chapman

Annie's story of her struggle with anger will help others learn how to conquer intense emotions, negative words, and angry actions. They will discover how to gain control and fix problems created by anger.

10 Things I Want My Daughter to Know
Annie Chapman

Drawing on years of motherhood, God's Word, and insights from women, Annie Chapman encourages you to share important truths with your daughters, including using choice to transform circumstances, depending on Jesus for strength and joy, and preparing for a successful marriage.

Mother-in-Law Dance
Annie Chapman

Believing that mothers-in-law and daughters-in-law can become close friends, Annie offers practical advice and biblical wisdom to help them nurture their relationship. Topics covered include dealing with traditions, handling intrusiveness, and coping with faith differences.

What Husbands and Wives Aren't Telling Each Other
Steve and Annie Chapman

Based on almost 500 surveys, Steve and Annie Chapman pinpointed communication problems in marriages. They use this information, their own experiences, and biblical principles to help readers create loving partnerships with open, satisfying communications.

STEVE AND ANNIE'S DISCOGRAPHY

At the Potter's House
Chapters
Coming Home for Christmas
An Evening Together
Family Favorites
For Times Like These
Kiss of Hearts
Long Enough to Know
A Mother's Touch
Never Turn Back
The Silver Bridge
This House Still Stands
Tools for the Trade
Waiting to Hear